VB Tips & Tricks

Volume One

David McCarter

PUBLISHED BY:

Mabry Publishing (an imprint of Mabry Software, Inc.)
Post Office Box 31926
Seattle, WA 98103-1926

Phone: 206-634-1443
Toll Free: 800-99-MABRY (U.S. only)
Fax: 206-632-0272

CompuServe: 71231,2066 or GO MABRY
Internet: mabry@mabry.com

WWW: http://www.mabry.com
FTP: ftp.mabry.com

Date of Printing: July 8, 1997

ISBN 1-890422-00-2 $24.95

Library of Congress Catalog Card Number: 97-71094

This book is dedicated to everyone that supported the newsletter by freely giving their best programming tips.

It's also dedicated to my family who have put up with me all these years while working on the newsletter.

-- David McCarter

Table Of Contents

Introduction

General Information

Welcome to the first in a series of books derived from the VB Tips & Tricks electronic newsletter. In its electronic version VB Tips & Tricks was first made available to the public in September of 1993. Since that time, this small underground newsletter has grown in popularity to where it's now downloaded an estimated 50,000 times each month (as of the printing of this book). It also comes with Visual Basic books, on the Mastering Visual Basic 4 training CD, the Visual Basic Programmers Journal CD and many more.

VB Tips & Tricks is the most powerful newsletter of its kind because it's written by programmers who are working "in the trenches" every day, just like you. It's full of real world solutions from real world programmers. It is not written by professional writers or editors who would not know how to program and deliver a professional application if their lives depended on it.

Why A Book?

So now, after all these years, why are we printing a book? Simple: because of the demand. Many years ago I started to receive messages from readers who wanted a printed version. At first I scratched my head and wondered why. The electronic version to me was ideal… it had searching capabilities, you could copy code right out of it and put it into your program… I just did not understand why. Those same readers told me they wanted "something to read on a plane", something they could "throw in their briefcase", something to read while "on vacation" and so on.

As you are well aware, the software world changes quickly. I wanted the VB Tips & Tricks books to keep up with it. Most books that are published are out of date the day they hit the streets. With each volume of the VB Tips & Tricks books, we will keep you on top of the latest happenings in the Visual Basic world. It's a good world to be in.

Focus Of This Volume

The focus of this first volume will be mostly Visual Basic 3.0, Windows 3.1 and some Visual Basic 4.0 and Windows 95. With Visual Basic 5.0 coming out in March of 1997, why would we do this? Easy, there are still scores of programmers using Visual Basic 3.0 and they will continue to do so for some time to come. So this volume will take the best of these types of tips from the newsletter.

Future volumes will concentrate more fully on the newer versions of Visual Basic.

Disks

In the back of this book, you will find two disks. The electronic version of VB Tips & Tricks is contained on these disks. Just run the SETUP.EXE file and enjoy.

How To Use The Tips

All the tips in this book have been fully tested and should work in most projects. Before you add code from a tip to your project, *save it first!*

If you do not want to type the code into your project, you can copy it out of the electronic version of the newsletter contained on the disks that came with this book.

All the tips are labeled with the version of Visual Basic on which they have been tested. Simply changing variable types and API calls can change just about any tip from one version of Visual Basic to the other.

How To Contact The Author

You can contact David McCarter via Internet e-mail at dpmcs@cts.com. Or, you can write him on CompuServe at 74227,1557.

You can visit his (VB Tips & Tricks) web site at http://www.apexsc.com/vb/nw/vbtt.html

Chapter 1

Hot Tips For Beginners

This chapter focuses mainly on general tips for new Visual Basic programmers. These "oldie but goodie" tips will help you overcome problems that seasoned programmers know in their sleep.

This chapter contains such popular tips as:

- Selecting text in a Text Box

- Detecting if a program is already running

- Filling Combo Boxes from a database

- Text encryption

- Parsing text strings

And more too! You will find that you'll use these tips over and over again.

Automatic Selection Of Text

Compatible With   **All Versions of Visual Basic**
Applies To   **Text Box, Combo Box**

When using edit boxes, it is often useful to generate automatic selection of text for your users when the control gets focus. This makes it easy to overwrite the text. You can do this easily by adding a couple of lines to the GotFocus event procedure:

```
Sub Text1_GotFocus ()
    Text1.SelStart = 0
    Text1.SelLength = 65535
End Sub
```

Notice that the length value for SelLength is 65535, the maximum length allowed in a Text Box. This forces Visual Basic to use the actual length of the text as the SelLength.

Activate Currently Running Instance

Compatible With   **All Versions of Visual Basic**
Applies To   **Application**

This code will activate the running instance of the program. To use this technique you must know the Caption of the program's main Form.

```
If App.PrevInstance Then
    AppActivate "MyApp Version 1.0"
    End
End If
```

Warn The User Of a Previous Instance

Compatible With   Visual Basic 3.0
Applies To   Application

The code will warn the user that they already have the program running

```
If App.PrevInstance Then
    sMsg = App.EXEName & " already running! "
    MsgBox sMsg, 4112
    End
End If
```

Disabling The Text Box Beep

Compatible With   All Versions of Visual Basic
Applies To   Text Box

Normally, the Text Box control will beep when the user presses the Enter key. This
behavior can be annoying, especially when you're using the Enter key to tab from one Text
Box to the next. Here's an easy way to disable the Text Box beep.

```
Sub Text1_KeyPress (KeyAscii As Integer)
    If KeyAscii = 13 Then  '13 is Key_Return
        KeyAscii = 0 '0 is nothing
    End If
End Sub
```

Easy String Encryption Using A Password

Compatible With   **All Versions of Visual Basic**
Applies To   **Strings**

There are many algorithms available for string encryption and decryption, but often they become complicated due to the need to ensure that the ASCII value of an encrypted character stays within the limits of a single byte (0-255). An elegant approach is to use the XOR function. The simple subroutine below will always give results falling within the 0-255 limit. It also has the advantage that a second call will reverse the encryption automatically.

```
Function Encrypt(sPassWord As String, sText As String) _
        As String
Dim I As Integer
Dim iPChar As Integer
Dim iCChar As Integer
    Do While Len(sPassWord) < Len(sText)
        sPassWord = sPassWord & sPassWord
    Loop
    For I = 1 To Len(sText)
        iPChar = Asc(Mid$(sPassWord, I, 1))
        Char = Asc(Mid$(sText, I, 1))
        d$(sText, I, 1) = Chr$(iPChar Xor iCChar)
    Next I
    Encrypt = sText
End Function
```

One thing you should be aware of is that the encrypted string may contain Chr$(0) values. While this will not be a problem with Visual Basic strings, other Windows objects treat Chr$(0) as an end-of-string character. Use of the encrypted string with a Text Box or in API calls may produce unexpected results.

Image Control As A Button

Compatible With   **All Versions of Visual Basic**
Applies To   **Image Control**

One of the easiest techniques for adding graphical effects to your program is to use image controls as a button. The key to this technique is to define a pair of invisible image controls with pictures corresponding to the up and down status of the control.

For example, you could create a button that visually represents a locked and unlocked state. When the Form is loaded, the Form_Load event procedure sets the appropriate image in the image control:

```
Sub Form_Load()
    Padlock.Picture = LockOpen.Picture
End Sub
```

The image control responds to the click event by replacing the picture in the control:

```
Sub Padlock_Click()
Static LockedFlag As Integer
    If LockedFlag Then
        Padlock.Picture = LockOpen.Picture
Else
            Padlock.Picture = LockClosed.Picture
    End If
    LockedFlag = Not LockedFlag
End Sub
```

You could also use a Picture control, but these controls take up much more resources than an Image control.

You can also use icons instead of bitmaps as the pictures. One advantage of using icon files rather than bitmap files is that any underlying image shows through the mask area of the icon. This gives a transparent effect as seen in Internet Explorer and other recent Microsoft programs.

Parse Text String And Fill An Array

Compatible With   **All Versions of Visual Basic**
Applies To   **Strings**

This routine can be used to parse a passed string and fill the passed dynamic array with the values.

Parameters

- sTextIn - The string to parse.

- sDelim - The delimiter (may be of variable length)

- aValues() - A dynamic array (un-dimensioned). When the function returns, this array will contain the parsed string fragments. Since the array is passed by reference (the Visual Basic default), it can be used by the calling procedure. If the array was passed ByVal, the calling procedure would not be able to use the values filled into the array and this routine would be worthless.

Return Value

Number of elements in the array.

Routine

```
Function iParseAndFillArray (sTextIn As String, _
        sDelim As String, aValues() As String) As Integer
    Dim iArrCt As Integer
    Dim iCurPos As Integer
    Dim iLenAssigned As Integer
    Dim iCurStrLen As Integer

    'Initilize counts
    iArrCt = 1
    iCurPos = 1
    iLenAssigned = 1
    'Get lenght of text to parse
    iCurStrLen = Len(sTextIn)
    Do
        'Re-allocate array keeping previous elements
        ReDim Preserve aValues(1 To iArrCt) As String
        'Get the current segment (not including delimiter)
```

```
            iCurStrLen = (InStr(iCurPos, sTextIn, sDelim) _
                - iCurPos)
        If iCurStrLen < 0 Then
            'If delimiter not found, we have the last
            'segment. Assign the value to array (the
            'last, righthand part)
            aValues(iArrCt) = Right$(sTextIn, _
                (Len(sTextIn) - (iLenAssigned - 1)))
            'Done!
            Exit Do
        Else
                'Assign the value to array
                aValues(iArrCt) = _
                    Mid$(sTextIn, iCurPos, iCurStrLen)
        End If
        'Assign start position of next element
        'Add length of current string to length assigned
        'var.
        iLenAssigned = iLenAssigned + _
            (Len(aValues(iArrCt)) + Len(sDelim))
        'Set the new starting position (ahead of current
        'delimiter) for next extraction
        iCurPos = iLenAssigned
        'Increment array index for next element
        iArrCt = iArrCt + 1
    Loop
    'Return # elements in array
    iParseAndFillArray = UBound(aValues)
End Function
```

Example

```
Dim sArray() As String
Dim R As Integer
R = iParseAndFillArray("VB|TIPS|&|TRICKS", "|", sArray())
```

NOTE: If the passed string ends with the delimiter, then there will be an extra array value filled with an empty string. To avoid this, remove the ending delimiter using the Left$ function before passing the string.

Set Focus To Running Instance

Compatible With   **All Versions of Visual Basic**
Applies To   **Application**

To activate and set focus to a minimized program or one that does not have focus, use the code below. You must know the Caption of the Form to use the following code.

```
Declare Function FindWindow Lib "User" (ByVal _
    lpClassName As Any, ByVal lpWindowName As Any) _
    As Integer
Declare Sub SFocus Lib "User" Alias "SetFocus" _
    (ByVal hwnd As Integer)


Dim sTitle As String
Dim hwnd As Integer
If App.PrevInstance Then
    hwnd = FindWindow(0&, "MyApp Version 1.0")
    If hwnd Then
        ShowWindow hwnd, 1
        SFocus hwnd                    'Sets focus
    End If
    End
End If
```

This code could also be used in the 32-bit version of Visual Basic by using the appropriate 32-bit API calls for FindWindow and SetFocus.

Filling Combo Boxes and List Boxes From A Database

Compatible With   **Visual Basic 4.0**
Applies To   **Combo Box, List Box**

You can use Combo Boxes and List Boxes in database apps and use these as lookup sources from other tables in the database. Here's a handy Class Module named ControlFill that you can use to fill the lists. Place this code in the General declaration section of the class module:

```
Option Explicit
```

```
Private SourceTable As Recordset
Private SourceFld As String
Private ControlType As Object
Private MyControl As Control

Public Function FillControl() As Boolean
    SourceTable.MoveFirst
    On Error GoTo ClassError
    If TypeOf MyControl Is ComboBox Or _
            TypeOf MyControl Is ListBox Then
        Do Until SourceTable.EOF
            MyControl.AddItem SourceTable(SourceFld)
            SourceTable.MoveNext
        Loop
        FillControl = True
        Else
            FillControl = False
    End If
    Exit Function
ClassError:
    MsgBox Err.Description
End Function

Public Property Let SourceControl(Source As Object)
    Set MyControl = Source
End Property

Public Property Let SourceField(Source As String)
    SourceFld = Source
End Property

Public Property Let SourceRS(Source As Recordset)
    Set SourceTable = Source
End Property
```

To use the code listed above, there are only three properties to set. Here is an example of using the class to fill several Combo Boxes (Control Array):

```
Dim dbData As Database
Dim I As Integer
Dim rsData as Recordset
Dim SelectCtrl As Object
```

```vb
Dim sDBPath As String
Dim CnrtFill As ControlFill

sDBPath = App.Path + "\lookups.mdb"
Set dbData = OpenDatabase(sDBPath)
Set rsData = dbData.OpenRecordset("Office")
Set CnrtFill = New ControlFill
'Set Recordset property for object
CnrtFill.SourceRS = rsData
'Set Field name for Object
CnrtFill.SourceField = "OfficeId"
For I = 0 To 5
    Set SelectCtrl = Combo1(I)
    'Send name of combo to Class object
    CnrtFill.SourceControl = Combo1(I)
    'Method used to fill the Combo
    If CnrtFill.FillControl = False Then
        MsgBox "Invalid Control Reference!"
    End If
Next I
```

Chapter 2 — Controls

This chapter contains a handy collection of tips that specifically deal with Visual Basic's standard controls. Some of what you will find included:

- Making controls look 3D in Windows 3.1

- Arranging items in a List Box

- Shadowing an control

- Using a List Box to move to a record in a database

- Creating custom tab stops.

Add Popup Menus To TreeView Controls

Compatible With   **Visual Basic 4.0 32-bit**
Applies To   **TreeView Control**

If you wanted to duplicate the functionality of the Windows Explorer in your application, using the Windows 95 TreeView control is the best way to do it. The problem is that the TreeView control does not support right click menus. There is no easy way to tell what mouse button was pushed to cause a NodeClick event.

The code below, when used in a TreeView MouseUp event, will capture the specific node that a right mouse button is clicked on, allowing you to popup a custom menu for that node.

Code

```
Private Sub TreeView1_MouseUp(Button As Integer, _
        Shift As Integer, x As Single, y As Single)
    Dim nod As Node

    If Button = vbRightButton Then
        Set nod = TreeView1.HitTest(x, y)
        On Error GoTo EmptyNode
        nod.Selected = True
        On Error GoTo 0
        '<<Customize menu here>>
        Me.PopupMenu mnuPopUp

    EmptyNode:
        On Error GoTo 0
    End If
End Sub
```

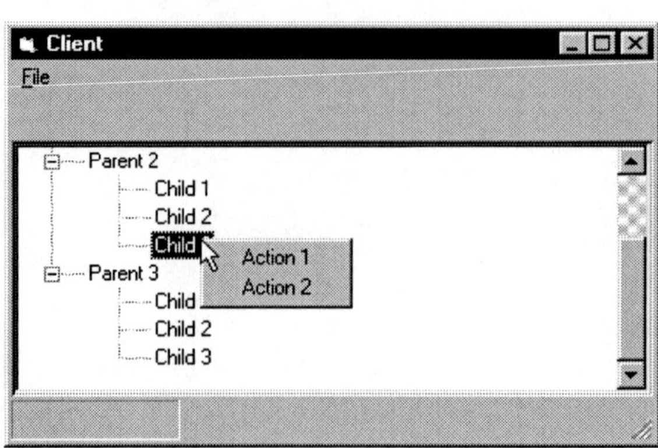

Create A Percent Bar

Compatible With   **All Versions of Visual Basic**
Applies To   **Picture Box**

Need a percent bar (or progress bar) for your program but don't want to add a VBX or OCX? Doing it with a PictureBox control is easy. Place a PictureBox onto your form, then set the DrawMode to 6 (Invert) and the AutoRedraw to True. Use the following code to draw the percent bar.

Code

```
Sub PerCnt(iNewValue As Integer)
    If iNewValue > 100 Or iNewValue < 0 Then
        Beep
        'Bad value, exit
        Exit Sub
    End If
    Picture1.Cls
    Picture1.FontSize = 12
    Picture1.ScaleMode = 0
    Picture1.ScaleWidth = 100
    Picture1.ScaleHeight = 10
    Picture1.CurrentY = 2
    Picture1.CurrentX = Picture1.ScaleWidth / 2 _
        - (Picture1.ScaleWidth / 15)
    Picture1.Print Str(iNewValue) & "%"
    Picture1.Line (0, 0)-(iNewValue, _
        Picture1.ScaleHeight), Picture1.FillColor, BF
End Sub
```

Usage

```
PerCnt CInt(Text1)
```

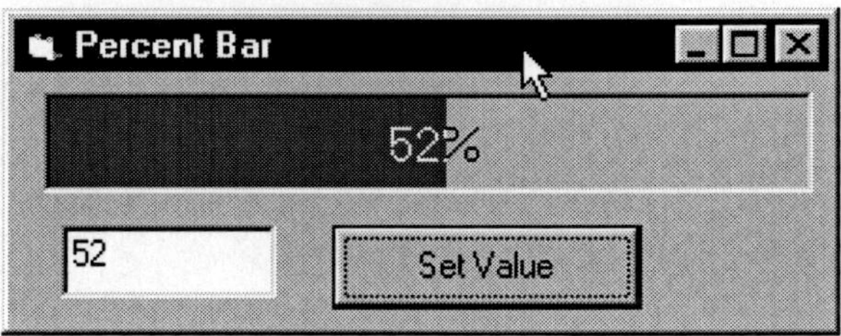

Create A Shadow Without Using A Control

Compatible With   **All Versions of Visual Basic**
Applies To   **Controls**

This subroutine draws a gray shadow below and to the right of a control.

Routine

```
Sub Shadow (fIn As Form, ctrlIn As Control)
    Const SHADOW_COLOR = &HC0C0C0
    Const SHADOW_WIDTH = 3
    Dim iOldWidth As Integer
    Dim iOldScale As Integer

    'Save the current DrawWidth and ScaleMode
    iOldWidth = fIn.DrawWidth
    iOldScale = fIn.ScaleMode

    fIn.ScaleMode = 3
    fIn.DrawWidth = 1

    'Draws the shadow around the control by drawing a gray
    'box behind the control that's offset right and down.
    fIn.Line (ctrlIn.Left + SHADOW_WIDTH, ctrlIn.Top + _
        SHADOW_WIDTH)-Step(ctrlIn.Width - 1, _
        ctrlIn.Height - 1), SHADOW_COLOR, BF

    'Restore Old Setting
    fIn.DrawWidth = iOldWidth
    fIn.ScaleMode = iOldScale
End Sub
```

Call this routine from the Form's Paint Subroutine. This routine works for Forms with a white BackGround. You can change the shadow color to any color you like.

Example

```
Shadow Me, Label1
```

Custom Tab Stops In A List Box

Compatible With   **Visual Basic 4.0**
Applies To   **List Box**

The List Box control provided in Visual Basic allows you to create a list of items, optionally sorted alphabetically. Each item can contain any type of ASCII characters, including control codes such as the tab character, and all items can be sorted if the Sort property of the List Box is set to True. However, when trying to add items separated by tabs, the output is not correctly formatted in two or more columns. This tip will explain how you can correctly format items in a List Box that contain embedded tab (ASCII 9) characters by using custom tab stop definitions in the standard List Box

Setting Tab Stops in List Boxes

If you've ever tried to align multiple columns of data in a List Box control, you'll know just how difficult this task can be. The data doesn't always line up properly (unless you have very short values for the columns). By using the following Windows API functions -- GetDialogBaseUnits and SendMessage -- you can add items to a List Box in correctly positioned columns.

To display text in columns using a List Box control, you must first obtain the dialog base units (more about these later), using the GetDialogBaseUnits API, that are currently in force. From this you can calculate the actual value required for each tab stop that you require in your List Box. The final step is to use SendMessage API to actually set the tab stops in the List Box to the desired positions. You can then add items with embedded tab characters to the List Box control and the output will be formatted correctly.

Dialog Box Base Units

A dialog box unit is a horizontal or vertical distance. One horizontal dialog box unit is equal to one-fourth of the current dialog box base width unit. The dialog box base units are computed based on the height and width of the current system font. The GetDialogBaseUnits function returns the current dialog box base units, in pixels.

Example Code

The example project to demonstrate custom tab stops in a List Box was developed and tested using Visual Basic 4.0 (both 16-bit and 32-bit). Visual Basic 3.0 users will have to pick out the relevant bits from the attached listings and ensure that each declare statement is on a single line, as Visual Basic 3.0 does not allow for the line continuation character.

Declare The Following

```
#If Win16 Then
    Declare Function GetDialogBaseUnits Lib "User" () _
        As Long
    Declare Sub SendMessage Lib "User" (ByVal hwnd _
        As Integer, ByVal wMsg As Integer, ByVal wParam _
        As Integer, lParam As Any)
#ElseIf Win32 Then
    Declare Function GetDialogBaseUnits Lib "user32" () _
        As Long
    Declare Function SendMessage Lib "user32" Alias _
        "SendMessageA" (ByVal hwnd As Long, ByVal wMsg _
        As Long, ByVal wParam As Long, lParam As Any) _
        As Long
#End If


#If Win16 Then
    Public Const WM_USER = &H400
    Public Const LB_SETTABSTOPS = (WM_USER + 19)
#ElseIf Win32 Then
    Public Const LB_SETTABSTOPS = &H192
#End If
```

Define the following Form level variables:

```
#If Win16 Then
    Dim iTabPos() As Integer 'Tab positions
#Else
    Dim lTabPos() As Long 'Tab positions
#End If
```

Code

The following procedure details the processing required to set custom tab stops in a standard List Box. This procedure works in Visual Basic 4.0 for both 16-Bit and 32-Bit.

```
Sub SetTabStops(lListWindowHandle As Long, iNoTabStops _
        As Integer, lTabPositions() As Long)
    '===========================================================
    'Parameter Definitions
    ' lListWindowHandle - List Box hWnd
    ' iNoTabStops       - Number of tabs wanted in the List Box.
```

```vba
' lTabPositions()  - An array of the tab positions required.
'==============================================================
    Dim iIndex As Integer      ' Index into array of
                                ' tab stops
    Dim lDialogBaseUnits As Long ' Dialog base units
    Dim iDialogUnitsX As Integer ' Horizontal dialog base
                                ' units


    'Obtain the dialog base units
    lDialogBaseUnits = GetDialogBaseUnits()
    iDialogUnitsX = (lDialogBaseUnits And &HFFFF&) / 4


    'Calculate the "required" tab positions
    #If Win16 Then
        ReDim iTabPos(0 To iNoTabStops - 1)
    #Else
        ReDim lTabPos(0 To iNoTabStops - 1)
    #End If


    For iIndex = 0 To iNoTabStops - 1
        #If Win16 Then
            iTabPos(iIndex) = lTabPositions(iIndex) _
                * iDialogUnitsX * 2
        #Else
            lTabPos(iIndex) = lTabPositions(iIndex) _
                * iDialogUnitsX * 2
        #End If
    Next iIndex


    'Set the required tab positions in the List Box,
    'by calling the "SendMessage" api and passing the
    'handle of the List Box and details of the number of
    'tabs and their positions.
    #If Win16 Then
        Call SendMessage(CInt(lListWindowHandle), _
            LB_SETTABSTOPS, iNoTabStops, iTabPos(0))
    #Else
        Call SendMessage(lListWindowHandle, _
            LB_SETTABSTOPS, CLng(iNoTabStops), lTabPos(0))
    #End If
End Sub
```

Example

Here is how you would set up your custom tabbed List Box.

```
Bach        Johann Sebastian   Germany
Barber      Samuel             United States
Beethoven   Ludwig van         Germany
Berlioz     Hector             France
Bernstein   Leonard            United States
Bizet       Georges            France
Brahms      Johannes           Germany
Britten     Benjamin           England
Chopin      Frederic           Poland
Debussy     Claude             France
Dvorak      Antonin            Czechoslovakia
```

```
#If Win16 Then
    Dim iListHandle As Integer 'List Box handle (16-Bit)
#Else
    Dim lListHandle As Long    'List Box handle (32-Bit)
#End If

Dim lTabPos(2) As Long          'Array of tab stops

    'Fill the tab position array
    lTabPos(0) = 15
    lTabPos(1) = 35
    lTabPos(2) = 45

    #If Win16 Then
        iListHandle = lstDisplay.hwnd
        Call SetTabStops(CLng(iListHandle), 3, lTabPos())
    #Else
        lListHandle = lstDisplay.hwnd
        Call SetTabStops(lListHandle, 3, lTabPos())
    #End If

    'Load the List Box data
    lstDisplay.Clear
    lstDisplay.AddItem "Bach" & Chr(9) & _
        "Johann Sebastian" & Chr(9) & "Germany"
    lstDisplay.AddItem "Barber" & Chr(9) & "Samuel" _
        & Chr(9) & "United States"
    lstDisplay.AddItem "Beethoven" & Chr(9) & "Ludwig van" _
```

```
               & Chr(9) & "Germany"
```

Fixing The Ampersand Problem

Compatible With   **All Versions of Visual Basic**
Applies To   **Controls that use Captions**

By default, if you use the "&" character in controls like a Label, Button or Form, it will actually put an underscore character under the next letter or number. This is used for creating ALT shortcut keys. While this is great for Menus, Tabs and some Command buttons there are many instances where you may not want this to happen. Here is an simple routine to fix that.

Code

```
Function sFixAmper (sStringToFix As String) As String
Dim sTemp As String
Dim iNum As Integer

    While InStr(sStringToFix, "&")
        iNum = InStr(sStringToFix, "&")
        sTemp = sTemp + Left$(sStringToFix, iNum) + "&"
        sStringToFix = Mid$(sStringToFix, iNum + 1)
    Wend
    sTemp = sTemp + sStringToFix
    sFixAmper = sTemp
End Function
```

Usage

```
Label2.Caption = sFixAmper(CStr(Label1.Caption))
```

Making Controls Look 3D

Compatible With   **Visual Basic 3.0**
Applies To   **Controls**

It's fairly easy to make your controls look 3D in Visual Basic 3.0. For controls that you want to look 3D, put "3D" (without the quotes) in the Tag property.. Call the following routine from the Form's Paint event.

Routine

```
Sub MakeControls3D (fIn As Form)
Dim lDarkGray As Long
Dim lFullWhite As Long
Dim I As Integer
Dim ITop As Integer
Dim ILeft As Integer
Dim IRight As Integer
Dim IBottom As Integer
Dim IDrawWidth As Integer
Dim ctrlName As Control

    lDarkGray = RGB(128, 128, 128)
    lFullWhite = RGB(255, 255, 255)
    IDrawWidth = fIn.DrawWidth
```

```
    'Set to the desiered width
    fIn.DrawWidth = 1
    'Loop thru controls on the Form
    For I = 0 To (fIn.Controls.Count - 1)
        Set ctrlName = fIn.Controls(I)
        If TypeOf ctrlName Is Menu Then
            'Skip Menu Items
        ElseIf InStr(UCase(ctrlName.Tag), "3D") <> 0 Then
            ITop = ctrlName.Top - Screen.TwipsPerPixelY
            ILeft = ctrlName.Left - Screen.TwipsPerPixelX
            IRight = ctrlName.Left + ctrlName.Width
            IBottom = ctrlName.Top + ctrlName.Height
            fIn.Line (ILeft, ITop)-(IRight, ITop), _
                lDarkGray
            fIn.Line (ILeft, ITop)-(ILeft, IBottom), _
                lDarkGray
            fIn.Line (ILeft, IBottom)-(IRight, _
                IBottom), lFullWhite
            fIn.Line (IRight, ITop)-(IRight, IBottom), _
                lFullWhite
        End If
    Next I
    'Set DrawWidth back the way we found it
    fIn.DrawWidth = IDrawWidth
End Sub
```

Example

```
Sub Form_Paint ()
    MakeControls3D Me
End Sub
```

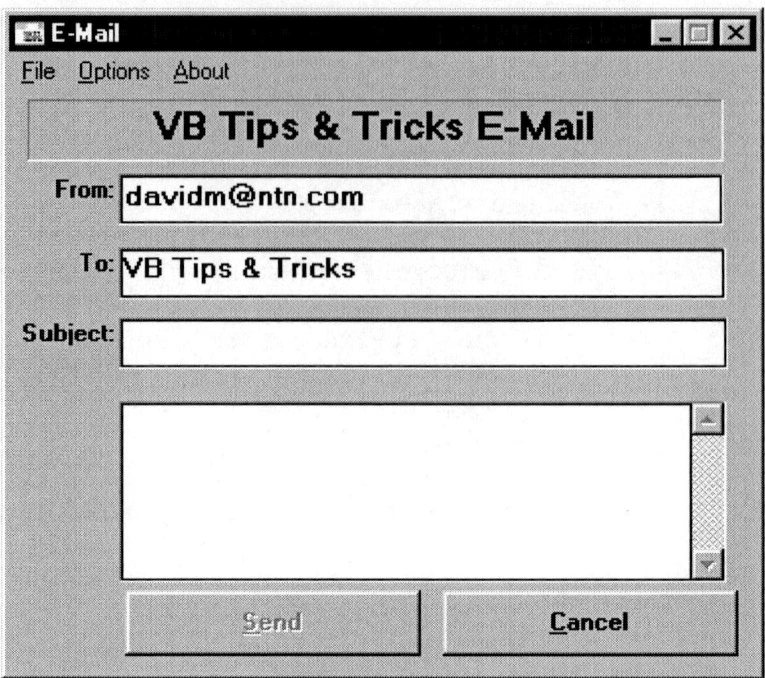

You can set the color and width of the effect to anything you desire. This routine looks better if the Form's BackGround color is set to gray. You could use this routine in Visual Basic 4.0 or Visual Basic 5.0, but they already have 3D capabilities built into them.

Centering The Mouse Pointer Over A Control

Compatible With   **Visual Basic 4.0**
Applies To   **Controls**

One nice user interface feature you might want to use in your program is to position the mouse cursor over a default control on a Form. This might be used most commonly with DialogBox type forms where the user needs to make a decision. Positioning the cursor over the button they will are likely to make the action quicker and easier.

The following code will center the mouse cursor over *any* control that has an hWnd property.

Declare

```vba
#If Win32 Then
    Type RECT
        left As Long
        top As Long
        right As Long
        bottom As Long
    End Type

    Declare Sub GetWindowRect Lib "User32" (ByVal hWnd As _
        Long, lpRect As RECT)
    Declare Sub SetCursorPos Lib "User32" (ByVal X As _
        Long, ByVal Y As Long)
#Else
    Type RECT
        left As Integer
        top As Integer
        right As Integer
        bottom As Integer
    End Type

    Declare Sub GetWindowRect Lib "User" (ByVal hWnd _
        As Integer, lpRect As RECT)
    Declare Sub SetCursorPos Lib "User" (ByVal X As _
        Integer, ByVal Y As Integer)
#End If
```

Code

```vba
Sub CenterCursor(hWnd As Long)
Dim rPosition As RECT
#If Win32 Then
    Dim X As Long
    Dim Y As Long
#Else
    Dim X As Integer
    Dim Y As Integer
#End If

    GetWindowRect hWnd, rPosition
```

```
      X = (rPosition.right + rPosition.left) / 2
      Y = (rPosition.bottom + rPosition.top) / 2
      SetCursorPos X, Y
End Sub
```

Usage

```
CenterCursor hWnd:=Command1.hWnd
```

Reducing Control Flicker

Compatible With   **All versions of Visual Basic**
Applies To   **Controls**

One of the thing that can make your control flicker and make your program look bad is changing properties that might not need to be changed. These properties are usually ones that cause the control to re-paint, like Enabled, Visible, Caption and Text. The flicker can be easily reduced by not setting a property when it is already set. For instance, if the Enabled property is set to True why set it to True again?

Enable/Disable Routine

Use this to enable or disable a control.

```
Sub SetEnabled (ctrlIn as Control, bSetting as Integer)
    If ctrlIn.Enabled <> bSetting Then
        ctrlIn.Enabled = bSetting
    End If
End Sub
```

Caption Routine

Use this to change a Caption property.

```
Sub SetLabel (ctrlIn as Control, sNewText as String)
    If ctrlIn.Caption <> sNewText Then
        ctrlIn.Caption = sNewText
    End If
End Sub
```

You can make as many of these types of routines as you like. Any property that affects a controls appearance, such as colors, fonts and text, would be a good prospect.

Rearrange Items In A List Box

Compatible With   **All Versions of Visual Basic**
Applies To   **Text Box, Combo Box**

Here's an easy way to allow for using the mouse to rearrange items in a List Box. Put a List Box named List1 on your Form. In the Declarations section of the Form, include the following:

```
Declare Function SendMessage Lib "User" (ByVal hWnd _
    As Integer, ByVal wMsg As Integer, ByVal wParam _
    As Integer, lParam As Any) As Long
Const WM_USER = &H400
Const LB_GETITEMHEIGHT = (WM_USER + 34)
Dim mintItemHeight As Integer
```

to account for different FontSize properties for the List Box, the Form_Load event should contain the following:

```
Sub Form_Load()
    mintItemHeight = Screen.TwipsPerPixelY *
    SendMessage(List1.hWnd, LB_GETITEMHEIGHT, 0, ByVal 0&)
End Sub
```

In the DragDrop event of the List Box, put this:

```
Sub List1_DragDrop (Source As Control, X As Single, Y _
        As Single)
    Dim intIndex As Integer, intRes As Integer, strItem As
    String

    strItem = List1.List(List1.ListIndex)
    intIndex = Y / mintItemHeight
    If intIndex > List1.ListCount Then
        List1.AddItem strItem
        Else
            List1.AddItem strItem, intIndex
    End If
```

```
      If List1.ListIndex >= 0 Then List1.RemoveItem
      List1.ListIndex
End Sub
```

In the MouseDown event of the List Box, type this:

```
Sub List1_MouseDown (Button As Integer, Shift As _
        Integer, X As Single, Y As Single)
    List1.Drag
End Sub
```

Finally, change the DragIcon property of the List Box to something appropriate, such as an icon in the VB\ICONS\DRAGDROP directory.

For a simple, added effect, you can let the user remove items from the List Box by dragging them to the Form. To do so, put this into the Form_DragDrop event:

```
Sub Form_DragDrop (Source As Control, X As Single, _
        Y As Single)
    If List1.ListIndex >= 0 Then
        List1.RemoveItem List1.ListIndex
    End If
End Sub
```

Furthermore, you can add code to the List1_DragDrop event to allow items to be dropped in it. You would need to check the source control by using its Tag property. For example, to determine which control is being dropped and what to do with it, this would be added before the List1_DragDrop code above:

```
If InStr(Source.Tag, "Label1") Then
    List1.AddItem Label1
Else
        strItem = List1.List(List1.ListIndex)
End If
```

This code requires the equivalent SendMessage 32-bit API call for Visual Basic 4.0 32-bit and Visual Basic 5.0.

Referencing A Control As A Global Variable

Compatible With Visual Basic 3.0
Applies To   Controls

Normally, referencing a control on another Form requires that the name of the Form containing the control be included in the reference as follows:

```
FormName!ControlName.PropertyName
```

Declaring a global Object variable to reference the control eliminates the need to include the FormName in the reference. Use the following code to create a global reference.

Place this code in the declarations section of a BAS module

```
Global MyGlobalName As ClassName
```

The ClassName of a control can be found in the properties list when the control name property is highlighted.

Place this code in the Form_Load event.

```
Set MyGlobalName = ControlName
```

ControlName is the name assigned to the control in the properties list.

The control may now be referenced from anywhere in the application as MyGlobalName.Property.

Example

```
Dim StatusLabel As Label
Set StatusLabel = Label1
```

Undo A Text Box or Combo Box

Compatible With	**Visual Basic 3.0, Visual Basic 4.0 16-bit**
Applies To	**Text Box, Combo Box**

For most controls, you will have to keep track of changes yourself. However, if you use the standard Text Box or Combo Box, Windows provides a "free" undo function for you!

Declare The Following

```
Declare Function SendMessage Lib "User" (ByVal hWnd _
    As Integer, ByVal wMsg As Integer, ByVal wParam _
    As Integer, lParam As Any) As Long
Global Const WM_USER = &h400
Global Const EM_UNDO = WM_USER + 23
```

Code

And in your Undo Sub, do the following:

```
UndoResult = SendMessage(myControl.hWnd, EM_UNDO, 0, 0)
```

Result of -1 indicates there was an error.

Using A List Box To Jump To A Record In A Database

Compatible With	**All Versions of Visual Basic**
Applies To	**List Box**

This is a simple and practical way to jump to a specific record when the user clicks on an entry in the List Box. Just use the ItemData property to associate a specific number with each item in the List Box.

Declare The Following

```
Dim bLoading as Integer
```

Code

```vb
Sub List1_Click( )
    Data1.Recordset.FindFirst "Number=" _
        + List1.ItemData(List1.ListIndex)
End Sub


Sub Form_Load ()
    'Set the global variable.
    bLoading = True
    'Open database & recordset.
    Data1.Refresh
    Do While Not Data1.Recordset.EOF
        'If not empty, then
        If Not IsNull(Data1.Recordset!Name) Then
            'Add to the list
            List1.AddItem Data1.Recordset!Name
            'When filling the List Box, also
            'fill the corresponding elements
            'In the ItemData with the 'employee' Numbers
            List1.ItemData(List1.NewIndex) = _
                Data1.Recordset!Number
        End If
        Data1.Recordset.MoveNext
    Loop
    'Rebuild the recordset.
    Data1.Refresh
    'Turn off global variable.
    Loading = False
End Sub


Sub Data1_Reposition ()
Dim I As Integer
    'If global variable is set.
    If Loading Then Exit Sub
    'Check items in List Box.
    For I = 0 To List1.ListCount - 1
        If list1.List( i ) = data1.Recordset!Name Then
            'Select matching item.
            List1.ListIndex = I
            'Stop looking through list.
```

```
            Exit For
        End If
    Next i
End Sub
```

Using DBList To Navigate Between Records

Compatible With   **Visual Basic 4.0**
Applies To   **DBList**

By using the DBList bound custom control which comes with Visual Basic 4.0, you can create a nice way of navigating through RecordSet. Here are the steps:

1. Use the Data Form Designer Add-Ins which come with Visual Basic 4.0 to create an entry screen from Biblio.MDB. Choose Publishers Table and all its of it and build the Form.

2. Create a new data control named Data2 by copying Data1 and pasting it onto the form. Set the properties ReadOnly = True and RecordSet = SnapShot,

3. Drop in a DBList Custom control, set the properties

```
DataSource = Data2 'This is different part, DataSource is
RowSource = Data2  'same as RowSource
DataField = PubID
'For we can access PubID from BoundText
BoundColumn = PubID
ListField = Company Name
```

4. Add in the code as following

```
'Change the position of Data1
Private Sub DBList1_Click()
    Data1.Recordset.FindFirst "pubid = " & DBList1.BoundText
End Sub


'Change the position of Data2 (which will control
'the DBList1)
Private Sub Data1_Reposition()
    'There is some code here generate by Data Form Designer
    ' Add this code in
```

```
        Data2.Recordset.FindFirst "pubid = " &
        Data1.Recordset("pubid")
    End Sub
```

5.   Run

6.   Click on the DBList items, Data1 will jump accordingly.

If you are using a normal List Box to achieve the same effect, you will need to use the AddItem method which will decrease performance significantly for large RecordSets. Using this approach, there is no to wait for all the data to come back from the database table.

Viewing A Large Picture Using Scroll Bars

Compatible With   **Visual Basic 4.0 32-bit**
Applies To   **PictureBox**

A common requirement is to be able to display a very large picture, one larger than the available screen space. You can buy add-on components to do this, but there is another way using just Visual Basic code.

Declare

```
#If Win32 Then
    Declare Function BitBlt Lib "gdi32" (ByVal hDestDC _
        As Long, ByVal X As Long, ByVal Y As Long, _
        ByVal nWidth As Long, ByVal nHeight As Long, _
        ByVal hSrcDC As Long, ByVal XSrc As Long, _
        ByVal YSrc As Long, ByVal dwRop As Long) As Long
#ElseIf Win16 Then
    Declare Function BitBlt Lib "GDI" (ByVal hDestDC _
        As Integer, ByVal X As Integer, ByVal Y As _
        Integer, ByVal nWidth As Integer, ByVal nHeight _
        As Integer, ByVal hSrcDC As Integer, ByVal XSrc _
        As Integer, ByVal YSrc As Integer, ByVal dwRop _
        As Long) As Integer
#End If


Public Const SRCCOPY = &HCC0020
```

Code

To create a demo on how this works, first create four controls and set them up as per the following settings:

Control 1

```
PictureBox
Name = picSrc
AutoRedraw = TRUE
AutoSize = TRUE
Picture = (bitmap)
ScaleMode = 3 - Pixel
Visible = FALSE
```

Control 2

```
PictureBox
Name = picDest
ScaleMode = 3 - Pixel
```

Control 3

```
VScrollBar
Name = VScr
Min = 0
Max = (number of vertical steps)
```

Control 4

```
HScrollBar
Name = HScr
Min = 0
Max = (number of horizontal steps)
```

Parent Form

```
Name = Form1
ScaleMode = 3 - Pixel
```

Then add the following subroutine to the form's code:

```
Sub UpdatePic ()
    Dim X
    X = bitblt(picDest.hDC, 0, 0, picDest.Width, _
```

```
          picDest.Height, picSrc.hDC, HScr.Value * _
          ((picSrc.Width - picDest.Width) / HScr.Max), _
          VScr.Value * ((picSrc.Height - picDest.Height) _
          / VScr.Max), SRCCOPY)
    End Sub
```

And add call of this routine to following events: VScr_Scroll, VScr_Change, HScr_Scroll, HScr_Change, picDest_Paint, Form_Resize.

```
    Private Sub Form_Resize()
        UpdatePic
    End Sub


    Private Sub HScr_Change()
        UpdatePic
    End Sub


    Private Sub HScr_Scroll()
        UpdatePic
    End Sub


    Private Sub picDest_Paint()
        UpdatePic
    End Sub


    Private Sub VScr_Change()
        UpdatePic
    End Sub


    Private Sub VScr_Scroll()
        UpdatePic
    End Sub
```

Your finished scrolling PictureBox will look like this:

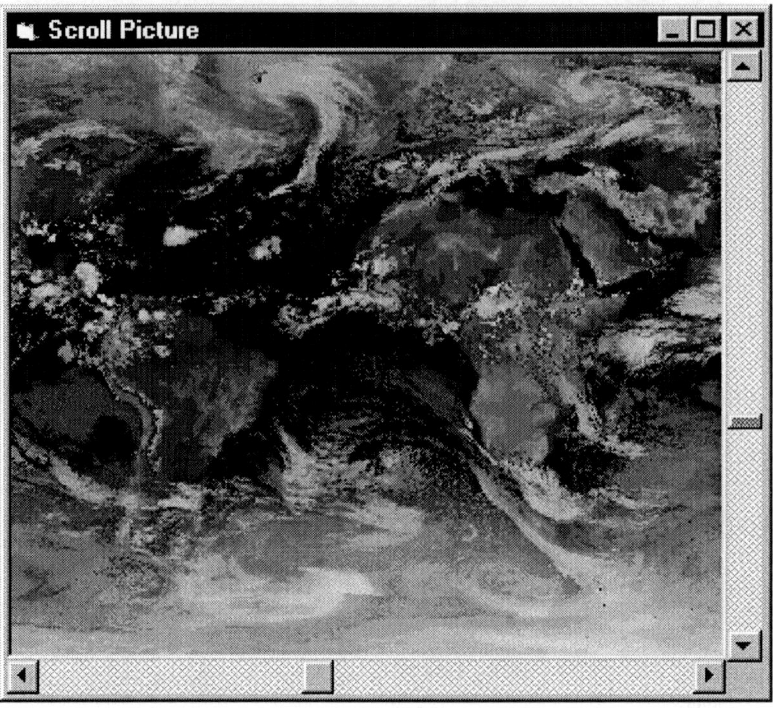

Chapter 3 — Disk And File Tips

The tips in this chapter deal with disks and files on a user's system. Visual Basic has never supported these two subjects very well, so you need to do things the hard way. Some tips include:

- Creating a nested directory

- Formatting a floppy disk

- Deleting files to the Windows 95 Recycling Bin

- Open a file with the COMMDLG.DLL

Check For An Existing File

Compatible With   **All Versions of Visual Basic**
Applies To   **Files**

Visual Basic doesn't provide a function to verify if a file exists, but you can use the Dir$ function for this purpose. The following code shows how you can easily implement your own FileExists function. You must trap errors in the event that an invalid drive is specified.

```
Function bFileExists(sFileName As String) As Integer
    Dim I As Integer
    On Error Resume Next
    I = Len(Dir$(sFileName))
    If Err Or I = 0 Then
        bFileExists = False
    Else
        bFileExists = True
    End If
End Function
```

Convert Long Files Names To Short File Names

Compatible With   **Visual Basic 4.0 32-bit**
Applies To   **Files**

Now that Microsoft has given us the ability to save long file names, there could be instances in your program that you might need to find out its short file name. The most likely reason is to use that file in a 16-bit program. It's simple with the following code.

Declare The Following

```vb
Private Declare Function GetShortPathName Lib "KERNEL32" _
    Alias "GetShortPathNameA" (ByVal lpszLongPath As _
    String, ByVal lpszShortPath As String, ByVal _
    cchBuffer As Long) As Long
```

Code

```vb
Public Function sGetShortFileName(ByVal FileName As _
        String) As String
    Dim lRC As Long
    Dim sShortPath As String
    Const PATH_LEN& = 164
    sShortPath = String$(PATH_LEN + 1, 0)
    lRC = GetShortPathName(FileName, sShortPath, PATH_LEN)
    sGetShortFileName = Left$(sShortPath, lRC)
End Function
```

Example

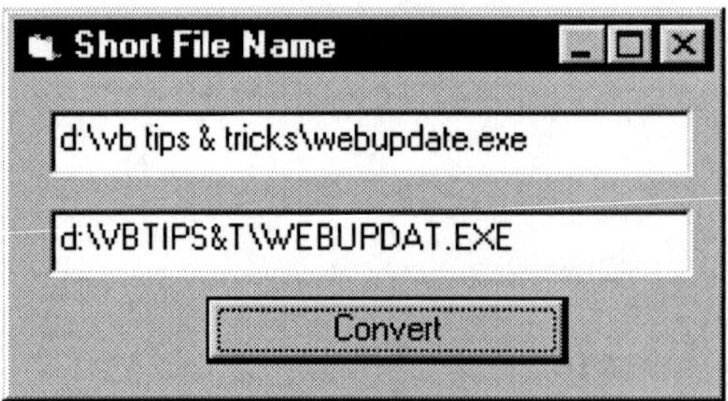


```vb
Private Sub Command1_Click()
    Text2.Text = sGetShortFileName(FileName:=Text1.Text)
End Sub
```

Create A Temporary File

Compatible With   **Visual Basic 4.0 32-bit**
Applies To   **Files**

Need a temporary file for your program to use? The 32-bit API has a call that will create a unique file for you in the Windows temporary directory.

Declare

```
Declare Function OSGetTempPath& Lib "kernel32" Alias _
    "GetTempPathA" (ByVal BufferLength&, ByVal Result$)
Declare Function OSGetTempFilename& Lib "kernel32" Alias _
    "GetTempFileNameA" (ByVal FilePath$, ByVal Prefix$, _
    ByVal wUnique&, ByVal TempFileName$)
```

Code

```
Function sGetTempFile(ByRef sPrefix As String)
    Dim sFilePath As String
    Dim sTempResult As String
    Dim lCharCount As Long
    Const MAX_RETURN = 3000

    sTempResult = Space$(MAX_RETURN)
    lCharCount = OSGetTempPath&(MAX_RETURN, sTempResult)
    sFilePath = Left$(sTempResult, lCharCount)

    sTempResult = Space$(MAX_RETURN)
    lCharCount = OSGetTempFilename&(sFilePath, sPrefix, _
        0, sTempResult)
    sGetTempFile = Left$(sTempResult, lCharCount)
End Function
```

Usage

```
sTempFile = sGetTempFile(sPrefix:="VBT")
```

This API call will tag a prefix (up to 3 characters) to the file. This makes it easier for you find, use, or delete your temporary files.

NOTE: Windows will NOT automatically delete these temporary files. So be kind to your user, keep track of them and delete them when the application closes.

How To Get A Disk's Serial Number

Compatible With   **Visual Basic 4.0 32-bit**
Applies To   **Disk**

As you might know DOS writes a serial number on a disk (hard disk or floppy disk) after it has been formatted. The serial number is not guaranteed to be unique, but since it's a 32-bit integer it's very unlikely you will find a duplicate. Many programmers use this serial number to copy-protect their programs. Under Windows 3.1 you would have to purchase a DLL to do this in Visual Basic. Well not any more! Microsoft has finally put it into the Win95 and WinNT Kernel API. To get a disks serial number do the following:

Declare The Following

```
Private Declare Function GetVolumeInformation _
    Lib "kernel32.dll" Alias "GetVolumeInformationA" _
    (ByVal lpRootPathName As String, ByVal _
    lpVolumeNameBuffer As String, ByVal nVolumeNameSize _
    As Integer, lpVolumeSerialNumber As Long, _
    lpMaximumComponentLength As Long, lpFileSystemFlags _
    As Long, ByVal lpFileSystemNameBuffer As String, _
    ByVal nFileSystemNameSize As Long) As Long
```

Code

```
Function GetSerialNumber(sRoot As String) As Long
    Dim lSerialNum As Long
    Dim R As Long
    Dim sTemp1 As String, sTemp2 As String
    sTemp1 = String$(255, Chr$(0))
    sTemp2 = String$(255, Chr$(0))
    R = GetVolumeInformation(sRoot, sTemp1, Len(sTemp1), _
        lSerialNum, 0, 0, sTemp2, Len(sTemp2))
    GetSerialNumber = lSerialNum
End Function
```

Usage

The Function will return an 0 if it the drive does not exist. You can pass it a directory name too, but if it does not exist, then it will also return a 0. To use, simply call:

```
lSerial = GetSerialNumber("c:\")
```

Creating A Nested Directory

Compatible With   **All Versions of Visual Basic**
Applies To   **Disk Directory**

If you want to create a directory with Visual Basic more than one layer deep you first must make sure that the directories above it exist. For example, the directory PROJECT directory in C:\TEMP\FINAL\PROJECT can not be created until the TEMP then the FINAL directories are created first.

Even though this code is relatively simple, it's surprising to see the number of major applications on the shelves that fail to correctly handle this scenario.

The code shown below consists of two functions. The bValDIR function is needed because in Visual Basic, if you try to create a directory using the MkDir function that already exists, MkDir will generate an error.

```
Sub MakeDir (sDirName As String)
Dim iMouseState As Integer
Dim iNewLen As Integer
Dim iDirLen As Integer
'Get Mouse State
    iMouseState = Screen.MousePointer
    'Change Mouse To Hour Glass
    Screen.MousePointer = 11
    'Set Start Length To Search For [\]
    iNewLen = 4

    'Add [\] To Directory Name If Not There
    If Right$(sDirName, 1) <> "\" Then
        sDirName = sDirName + "\"
    End If

    'Create Nested Directory
    Do While Not bValDir(sDirName)
        iDirLen = InStr$(iNewLen, sDirName, "\")
        If Not bValDir(Left$(sDirName, iDirLen)) Then
            MkDir Left$(sDirName, iDirLen - 1)
        End If
        iNewLen = iDirLen + 1
    Loop

    'Leave The Mouse The Way You Found It
```

```
      Screen.MousePointer = iMouseState
End Sub


Function bValDir (sIncoming As String) As Integer
Dim iCheck As String
Dim iErrResult As Integer
On Local Error GoTo ValDirError
    If Right$(sIncoming, 1) <> "\" Then
        sIncoming = sIncoming + "\"
    End If
    iCheck = Dir$(sIncoming)
    If iErrResult = 76 Then
        bValDir = False
    Else
        bValDir = True
    End If
    Exit Function
ValDirError:
    Select Case Err
        Case Is = 76
            iErrResult = Err
            Resume Next
        Case Else
    End Select
End Function
```

Formatting A Floppy Disk

Compatible With   **Visual Basic 3.0**
Applies To   **Disk**

There is no easy way to format a floppy disk in Windows 3.1. The following solution is not elegant, but it seems the only way to go unless you use a specially written DLL . Microsoft should have given developers access to this kind of function through the File Manager. Oh, well...

The best way to format a disk is to use DOS (our old friend). Here are some tips.

- Make sure that the disk is a floppy (removable) disk!

- To make things faster, use the Quick Format option available from DOS 5.0 and above.

Declare The Following

```
Declare Function WinExec Lib "Kernel" (ByVal lpCmdLine _
    As String, ByVal nCmdShow As Integer) As Integer
Declare Function GetNumTasks Lib "Kernel" () As Integer
Declare Function GetDriveType Lib "Kernel" (ByVal nDrive As
    Integer) As Integer
Declare Function GetTempFileName Lib "Kernel" _
    (ByVal cDriveLetter As Integer, ByVal lpPrefixString _
    As String, ByVal wUnique As Integer, ByVal _
    lptempfilename As String) As Integer
Declare Function GetVersion Lib "Kernel" () As Long
```

Use the following Function:

```
Function iFormatFloppyDisk (sDriveLetter As String, _
        sVolumeName As String) As Integer
    Dim sCommand As String
    Dim sTempFile As String
    Dim iFileNum As Integer
    Dim iReturn As Integer
    Dim iActiveApps As Integer
    Dim sQuickFormat As String
    Dim X As Integer
    Const SW_HIDE = 0

    'MakeSure that the drive if removable
    If GetDriveType(Asc(Left(sDriveLetter, 1)) - 65) _
            <> 2 Then
        FormatFloppyDisk = False
        Exit Function
    End If

    'Format Driveletter
    sDriveLetter = Left$(sDriveLetter, 1) & ":"

    'If 5.0 or Higher Use Quick Format
    If Val(sGetDosVer()) >= 5 Then
        sQuickFormat = "/Q"
    Else
        sQuickFormat = ""
```

```vb
    End If

    'Get Temp File Name
    sTempFile = sGetTempFile("FFD")

    'Create Input File (for hands-off operation)
    sCommand = Chr(13) & Chr(10) & Chr(13) & Chr(10) & "N" _
        & Chr(13) & Chr(10)
    iFileNum = FreeFile
    Open sTempFile For Output As #iFileNum
    Print #iFileNum, sCommand
    Close #iFileNum

    'Format Disk
    iActiveApps = GetNumTasks()
    iReturn = WinExec("doswin.pif /c c:\dos\format " & _
        sDriveLetter & " /v:" & sVolumeName & sQuickFormat _
        & "/u <" & sTempFile, SW_HIDE)
    Do While GetNumTasks() <> iActiveApps
        X = DoEvents()
    Loop

    'Get Rid Of The Temp File
    Kill sTempFile

    'Return WinExec Value (any value above 32
    'means success!)
    iFormatFloppyDisk = iReturn
End Function

Function sGetTempFile (sPrefix As String) As String
    Dim sTempFileName As String
    Dim R As Integer

    sTempFileName = Space$(144)

    R = GetTempFileName(ByVal 0, ByVal sPrefix, _
        ByVal 0, ByVal sTempFileName)

    sGetTempFile = Mid$(sTempFileName, 1, _
        Len(Trim$(sTempFileName)) - 1)
```

```
End Function

Function sGetDosVer () As String
    Dim lVer As Long
    Dim lDosVer As Long

    lVer = GetVersion()
    lDosVer = CInt(lVer / &H10000)
    sGetDosVer = Format$(lDosVer / 256) + "." _
        + Format$(lDosVer And &HFF)
End Function
```

If this Function returns a value greater than 32, then everything went well. If you don't want your users to see the DOS screen while the formatting takes place, create a PIF file called DOSWIN.PIF and set Display Usage set to Windowed.

How To Delete A File to the Win95 Recycling Bin

Compatible With   **Visual Basic 4.0 32-bit**
Applies To   **Files**

Visual Basic 4.0 applications under Window 95 or Windows NT can call the Win32 API's SHFileOperation function to delete a file to the Windows 95 Recycling Bin. Users quickly become accustomed to using new operating system features such as the recycling bin and may be disappointed if they find that your programs do not support them.

Declare The Following

```
Type SHFILEOPSTRUCT
    hWnd As Long
    wFunc As Long
    pFrom As String
    pTo As String
    fFlags As Integer
    fAborted As Boolean
    hNameMaps As Long
    sProgress As String
End Type
Public Const FO_DELETE = &H3
Public Const FOF_ALLOWUNDO = &H40
```

```
Declare Function SHFileOperation Lib "shell32.dll" _
    Alias "SHFileOperationA" (lpFileOp As SHFILEOPSTRUCT) _
    As Long
```

Code

```
Public Function ShellDelete(ParamArray vntFileName() _
        As Variant)
    Dim I As Integer
    Dim sFileNames As String
    Dim SHFileOp As SHFILEOPSTRUCT

    For I = LBound(vntFileName) To UBound(vntFileName)
        sFileNames = sFileNames & _
            vntFileName(I) & vbNullChar
    Next I
    sFileNames = sFileNames & vbNullChar
    With SHFileOp
        .wFunc = FO_DELETE
        .pFrom = sFileNames
        .fFlags = FOF_ALLOWUNDO
    End With
    ShellDelete = SHFileOperation(SHFileOp)
End Function
```

Example

The function's ParamArray argument allows you to call it in several ways:

```
'Delete a single file
lResult = ShellDelete("setupwizard.exe")

'Pass file names in an array
sFileName(1) = "setupwizard.exe"
sFileName(2) = "setupwizard.hlp"
sFileName(3) = "setupwizard.doc"
lResult = ShellDelete(sFileName())

'Pass file names as parameters
lResult = ShellDelete("setupwizard.exe", _
    "setupwizard.hlp", "setupwizard.doc")
```

Opening A File With Its Associated Program

Compatible With   **Visual Basic 4.0 32-bit**
Applies To   **Disk**

There are many times when you want to open a file with the its associated program. For instance, you might want to display a Word DOC for or an Adobe PDF file. Normally, you would just run:

```
R = Shell("word.exe mydoc.doc")
```

But most of the time, you will not know where Word is installed. Simply writing

```
R = Shell("mydoc.doc")
```

won't work. The functionally of Shell in Visual Basic is very limited. Much greater functionality can be had by using the ShellExecute API call. The following code will open a file with its associated program:

Declare The Following

```
Private Declare Function ShellExecute Lib "shell32.dll" _
    Alias "ShellExecuteA" (ByVal hwnd As Long, ByVal _
    lpOperation As String, ByVal lpFile As String, _
    ByVal lpParameters As String, ByVal lpDirectory _
    As String, ByVal nShowCmd As Long) As Long
```

Code

```
ShellExecute hwnd:=Screen.ActiveForm.hwnd, _
    lpOperation:="Open", lpFile:="mydoc.doc", _
    lpParameters:=vbNullString, lpDirectory:="c:\myapp", _
    nShowCmd:=vbNormalFocus
```

Parameter	Description
hwnd	Identifies the parent window. This window receives any message boxes produced by an application (for example, for error reporting).
LpOperation	Points to a null-terminated string specifying the operation to perform. This string can be "open" or "print." If this parameter is NULL, "open" is the default value.
LpFile	Points to a null-terminated string specifying the file to open.
LpParameters	Points to a null-terminated string specifying parameters passed to the application when the lpFile parameter specifies an executable file. If lpFile points to a string specifying a document file, this parameter is NULL.
LpDirectory	Points to a null-terminated string specifying the default directory.
NShowCmd	Specifies whether the application window is to be shown when the application is opened. This parameter can be one of the values described in the API ShowWindow().

Using COMMDLG.DLL To Open A File

Compatible With   **Visual Basic 3.0**
Applies To   **Files**

If you use the CMDIALOG.VBX to let the user open files, you can save memory, and shipping the VBX, by using COMMDLG.DLL directly!

Declare The Following

```
Type tagOPENFILENAME
    lStructSize As Long
    hwndOwner As Integer
    hInstance As Integer
    lpstrFilter As Long
    lpstrCustomFilter As Long
    nMaxCustFilter As Long
    nFilterIndex As Long
    lpstrFile As Long
    nMaxFile As Long
```

```
        lpstrFileTitle As Long
        nMaxFileTitle As Long
        lpstrInitialDir As Long
        lpstrTitle As Long
        Flags As Long
        nFileOffset As Integer
        nFileExtension As Integer
        lpstrDefExt As Long
        lCustData As Long
        lpfnHook As Long
        lpTemplateName As Long
End Type

Declare Function GetOpenFileName% Lib "COMMDLG.DLL" _
    (OPENFILENAME As tagOPENFILENAME)
Declare Function GetSaveFileName% Lib "COMMDLG.DLL" _
    (OPENFILENAME As tagOPENFILENAME)
Declare Function lstrcpy& Lib "Kernel" (ByVal _
    lpDestString As Any, ByVal lpSourceString As Any)

Dim OpenFileName As tagOPENFILENAME

Global Const OFN_READONLY = &H1
Global Const OFN_OVERWRITEPROMPT = &H2
Global Const OFN_HIDEREADONLY = &H4
Global Const OFN_NOCHANGEDIR = &H8
Global Const OFN_SHOWHELP = &H10
Global Const OFN_ENABLEHOOK = &H20
Global Const OFN_ENABLETEMPLATE = &H40
Global Const OFN_ENABLETEMPLATEHANDLE = &H80
Global Const OFN_NOVALIDATE = &H100
Global Const OFN_ALLOWMULTISELECT = &H200
Global Const OFN_EXTENSIONDIFFERENT = &H400
Global Const OFN_PATHMUSTEXIST = &H800
Global Const OFN_FILEMUSTEXIST = &H1000
Global Const OFN_CREATEPROMPT = &H2000
Global Const OFN_SHAREAWARE = &H4000
Global Const OFN_NOREADONLYRETURN = &H8000
Global Const OFN_NOTESTFILECREATE = &H10000

Global Const OFN_SHAREFALLTHROUGH = 2
```

```vb
Global Const OFN_SHARENOWARN = 1
Global Const OFN_SHAREWARN = 0

Function OpenCommDlg (sFilter As String, sDefExt As _
    String, sCurDir As String, sTitle As String) As String

' sFilter is the dropdown of file types (leave blank for
'   defaults)
' sDefExt is used if the user does not specify an extension
' sCurDir is the default directory
' sTitle is the dialog title

Dim sMessage As String
Dim sFileName As String
Dim sFileTitle As String
Dim iAPIResults As Integer

    If sFilter = "" Then
        sFilter = "All Files(*.*)" & Chr$(0) & "*.*" _
            & Chr$(0)
        sFilter = sFilter & "Text(*.txt)" & Chr$(0) _
            & "*.TXT" & Chr$(0)
        sFilter = sFilter & "Program Files" & Chr$(0) _
            & "*.EXE;*.COM;*.BAT;*.PIF" & Chr$(0)
        sFilter = sFilter & Chr$(0)
    Else
        sFilter = sFilter & Chr$(0)
    End If

    'Allocate string space for the returned strings.
    sFileName = Chr$(0) & Space$(255) & Chr$(0)
    sFileTitle = Space$(255) & Chr$(0)

    'Give the dialog a caption title.
    sTitle = sTitle & Chr$(0)

    'Set the default extension
    sDefExt = sDefExt & Chr$(0)

    'Set up the default directory
    If Len(sCurDir) = 0 Then
```

```vb
        sCurDir = CurDir$ & Chr$(0)
Else
        sCurDir = sCurDir & Chr$(0)
End If


'Set up the data structure before you call the
'GetOpenFileName
OPENFILENAME.lStructSize = Len(OPENFILENAME)


'If the OpenFile Dialog box is linked to a Form use
'this line. It will pass the forms window handle.

OPENFILENAME.hwndOwner = Screen.ActiveForm.hWnd


'If the OpenFile Dialog box is not linked to any Form
'use this line. It will pass a null pointer.

OPENFILENAME.hwndOwner = 0&


OPENFILENAME.lpstrFilter = lstrcpy(sFilter, sFilter)
OPENFILENAME.nFilterIndex = 1
OPENFILENAME.lpstrFile = lstrcpy(sFileName, sFileName)
OPENFILENAME.nMaxFile = Len(sFileName)
OPENFILENAME.lpstrFileTitle = lstrcpy(sFileTitle, _
    sFileTitle)
OPENFILENAME.nMaxFileTitle = Len(sFileTitle)
OPENFILENAME.lpstrTitle = lstrcpy(sTitle, sTitle)
OPENFILENAME.Flags = 0 ' OFN_FILEMUSTEXIST Or _
    OFN_READONLY
OPENFILENAME.lpstrDefExt = lstrcpy(sDefExt, sDefExt)
OPENFILENAME.hInstance = 0
OPENFILENAME.lpstrCustomFilter = 0
OPENFILENAME.nMaxCustFilter = 0
OPENFILENAME.lpstrInitialDir = lstrcpy(sCurDir, sCurDir)
OPENFILENAME.nFileOffset = 0
OPENFILENAME.nFileExtension = 0
OPENFILENAME.lCustData = 0
OPENFILENAME.lpfnHook = 0
OPENFILENAME.lpTemplateName = 0


'This will pass the desired data structure to the
```

```
    'Windows API, which will in turn it uses to display
    'the Open Dialog Form.

    iAPIResults = GetOpenFileName(OPENFILENAME)

    If iAPIResults <> 0 Then
        'Note that sFileName will have an embedded Chr$(0)
        'at the end. You may wish to strip this character
        'from the string.
        sFileName = Left$(sFileName, InStr(sFileName, _
            Chr$(0)) - 1)
        OpenCommDlg = sFileName
    Else
        OpenCommDlg = ""
    End If
End Function
```

Example

Usage would be as follows:

```
FileName = OpenCommDlg (Filter, DefaultExtension, _
    DefaultDirectory, Title)
```

Returns the selected file name including path. If the user gave no extension, then the default extension will be added to the end of the file.

Example 1

This simplest use of the OpenCommDlg function simply passes all blank parameters:

```
sFileName = OpenCommDlg ("","","","")
```

Example 2

Here is the most common way you might use this routine.

```
Sub Command1_Click ()
    Dim sFileName As String
    Dim sFilter As String
    Dim sDefaultExt As String
    Dim sDefaultDir As String
    Dim sCaption As String
```

```
        sFilter = "Word Files (*.doc)" & Chr$(0) & "*.doc" _
            & Chr$(0)
        sFilter = sFilter & "RTF Files (*.rtf)" & Chr$(0) _
            & "*.rtf" & Chr$(0)
        sDefaultExt = "doc"
        sCaption = "Save Document"
        sDefaultDir = App.Path

        sFileName = OpenCommDlg(sFilter, sDefaultExt, _
            sDefaultDir, sCaption)
End Sub
```

Chapter 4 — Forms

This chapter contains handy tips for working with Forms in Visual Basic. Most are very common, and you might use them in all of your projects. Some tips we will cover include:

- Centering a Form

- Keeping a Form on top of all other windows

- Properly unloading Forms

- Removing a Form's Title Bar

Waiting For A Form To Become Inactive

Compatible With   **All Versions of Visual Basic**
Applies To   **Forms**

Sometimes you might want to suspend your program until a Form has become inactive. This is a good idea when, for instance, you need a Form to re-paint.

Code

```
Sub FormWait (frmIn As Form)
    Do While frmIn Is Screen.ActiveForm
        DoEvents
    Loop
End Sub
```

Usage

```
FormWait frmMain
```

Centering A Form

Compatible With   **Visual Basic 4.0**
Applies To   **Forms**

Instead of having your Forms come up just anywhere on your user's screen, it's usually desirable to place them in the center. As a matter of fact, if you don't place them somewhere, they will come up in the same position as they were in Visual Basic design mode! If you use a higher screen resolution than your users, your forms could be partially hidden or even completely off the screen.

There are a few different ways to center your Forms and this tip is by far the best one. It's very useful because you can center your form over any other form. It's good to center status Form over your applications mail form instead of the Screen. It just looks nicer. This object can be another Form or the Screen.

Code

```
Sub CenterForm(objChild As Object, objParent As _
        Object, Optional vLeftTopOffset As Variant, _
        Optional vTopOffset As Variant, Optional vMode _
        As Variant)
    Dim iLeft As Integer
    Dim iTop As Integer
    Dim iMode As Integer
    Dim iLOffset As Integer
    Dim iTOffset As Integer
    Dim I As Integer

    If TypeOf objParent Is SysInfo Then
        iLeft = objParent.WorkAreaLeft + _
            (objParent.WorkAreaWidth - objChild.Width) / 2
        iTop = objParent.WorkAreaTop + _
            (objParent.WorkAreaHeight - objChild.Height) / 2
    ElseIf TypeOf objParent Is MDIForm Then
        If objChild.MDIChild = True Then
            iLeft = (objParent.ScaleWidth - _
                objChild.Width) / 2
            iTop = (objParent.ScaleHeight - _
                objChild.Height) / 2
        Else
            iLeft = objParent.Left + (objParent.Width - _
```

```
            objChild.Width) / 2
        iTop = objParent.Top + (objParent.Height - _
            objChild.Height) / 2
    End If
ElseIf TypeOf objParent Is Screen Then
    iLeft = (objParent.Width - objChild.Width) / 2
    iTop = (objParent.Height - objChild.Height) / 2
ElseIf TypeOf objParent Is Form Then
    If objParent.MDIChild = True Then
        iLeft = objParent.Left + (objParent.Width - _
            objChild.Width) / 2
        iTop = objParent.Top + (objParent.Height - _
            objChild.Height) / 2

        For I = 0 To Forms.Count - 1
            If TypeOf Forms(I) Is MDIForm Then
                iLeft = iLeft + (Forms(I).Width - _
                    Forms(I).ScaleWidth) / 2 + _
                    Forms(I).Left
                iTop = iTop + (Forms(I).Height - _
                    Forms(I).ScaleHeight) / 2 + _
                    Forms(I).Top
                Exit For
            End If
        Next I
    Else
        iLeft = objParent.Left + (objParent.Width - _
            objChild.Width) / 2
        iTop = objParent.Top + (objParent.Height - _
            objChild.Height) / 2
    End If
Else
    Exit Sub
End If


If IsMissing(vMode) Or objChild.MDIChild = True Then
    iMode = vbModeless
Else
    iMode = Int(vMode)
End If
```

```
    If IsMissing(vLeftTopOffset) Then
        iLOffset = 0
    Else
        iLOffset = Int(vLeftTopOffset)
    End If
    If IsMissing(vTopOffset) Then
        iTOffset = 0
    Else
        iTOffset = Int(vTopOffset)
    End If


    objChild.Move iLeft + iLOffset, iTop + iTOffset
    objChild.Show iMode
End Sub
```

Examples

Example 1

Center the Form on the Screen.

```
CenterForm objChild:=Me, objParent:=Screen
```

Example 2

Center the Form as Modal on the Screen.

```
CenterForm objChild:=Me, objParent:=Screen, vMode:=vbModal
```

Example 3

Center the Form on the Windows 95 viewing area (takes into account the TaskBar). This requires that a SysInfo control (which comes with Visual Basic) be placed on the Form.

```
CenterForm objChild:=Me, objParent:=SysInfo
```

Example 4

Centers the Form on a Parent Form.

```
CenterForm objChild:=Me, objParent:=frmMain
```

You can also use the vTopOffset and vLeftOffset parameters to center the Form and then add or subtract from the X and Y coordinates.

Keeping A Window On Top

Compatible With   **Visual Basic 3.0, Visual Basic 4.0 16-bit**
Applies To   **Forms**

There are times when you might want to make sure that one of your program's forms stay on top of all other windows. You can keep your window on top by using the code listed below.

Declare The Following

```
Declare Sub SetWindowPos Lib "User" (ByVal hwnd As Integer,
    ByVal hWndInsertAfter As Integer, ByVal x As Integer,
    ByVal y As Integer, ByVal cx As Integer, ByVal cy As
    Integer, ByVal wFlags As Integer)
Const SWP_NOMOVE = 2
Const SWP_NOSIZE = 1
Const HWND_TOPMOST = -1
Const HWND_NOTOPMOST = -2
```

Code

```
Sub KeepOnTop (frmIn As Form, bOnTop As Integer)
    Dim iTopFlag As Integer
    Const wFlags = SWP_NOMOVE Or SWP_NOSIZE

    If bOnTop = True Then
        iTopFlag = HWND_TOPMOST
    Else
        iTopFlag = HWND_NOTOPMOST
    End If
    SetWindowPos frmIn.hWnd, iTopFlag, 0, 0, 0, 0, wFlags
    DoEvents
End Sub
```

Usage

To put a Form on top of all windows, then call:

```
KeepOnTop Me, True
```

To remove the Form from being on top, call:

```
KeepOnTop Me, False
```

Unloading Forms

Compatible With   **Visual Basic 4.0**
Applies To   **Forms**

I've seen lot of tips on how to unload forms. The problem with these tips is that they do not take into account that the Sub might be called from the QueryUnload or Unload event of a Form. If it is, then the program will bomb because you cannot unload a Form that is already being, or has been, unloaded.

Code

```
Public Sub UnloadAllForms(sFormName As String)
Dim Form As Form
    For Each Form In Forms
        If Form.Name <> sFormName Then
            Unload Form
            Set Form = Nothing
        End If
    Next Form
End Sub
```

This simply uses the Forms collection to unload all the forms. It also uses "Set Form = Nothing" to make sure all the memory is released that the Form was using. If you are calling it from a Form, pass it the Form name. Here is an example:

```
Call UnloadAllForms Me.Name
```

If you call it from a Sub or Function, use:

```
Call UnloadAllForms ""
```

Notice that the sFormName is not optional. This way you won't forget to pass it the Form Name.

Removing A Form's Title Bar

Compatible With	**Visual Basic 3.0, Visual Basic 4.0 16-bit**
Applies To	**Form**

There might be times where you want to remove the title bar from a Form. The only way to do this is by using API calls. This routine will remove the title bar and also put it back. You might find this useful for creating dialog box type Forms.

Declare The Following

```
Declare Function GetWindowWord% Lib "User" (ByVal hWnd%, _
    ByVal nIndex%)
Declare Function SetWindowWord% Lib "User" (ByVal hWnd%, _
    ByVal nIndex%, ByVal wNewWord%)
Declare Function GetWindowLong& Lib "User" (ByVal hWnd%, _
    ByVal nIndex%)
Declare Function SetWindowLong& Lib "User" (ByVal hWnd%, _
    ByVal nIndex%, ByVal dwNewLong&)
Const GWW_ID = (-12)
Const GWL_STYLE = (-16)
Const WS_DLGFRAME = &H400000
Const WS_SYSMENU = &H80000
Const WS_MINIMIZEBOX = &H20000
Const WS_MAXIMIZEBOX = &H10000
```

Code

```
Sub ShowTitleBar (frmIn As Form, bShow As Integer)
    Static iOldMenu As Integer
    Static lSavedStyle As Long
    Dim lNewStyle As Long
    Dim R As Long

    If bShow Then
        'get the current style attributes
        lNewStyle = GetWindowLong&(frmIn.hWnd, GWL_STYLE)

        'set only the attributes that were removed earlier
        lNewStyle = lNewStyle Or lSavedStyle

        're-establish the menu
```

```
    If iOldMenu <> 0 Then
        R = SetWindowWord%(frmIn.hWnd, GWW_ID, iOldMenu)
    End If


    'set the new style
    R = SetWindowLong&(frmIn.hWnd, GWL_STYLE, lNewStyle)

    'force Visual Basic to update the Form
    frmIn.Move frmIn.Left
    frmIn.Refresh
Else
    'get the current style attributes
    lNewStyle = GetWindowLong&(frmIn.hWnd, GWL_STYLE)

    'determine whether the Form has a dialog frame,
    'a ControlBox, a minimize button, or a maximize
    'button and save this info for later use
    lSavedStyle = 0
    lSavedStyle = lSavedStyle Or (lNewStyle And _
        WS_DLGFRAME)
    lSavedStyle = lSavedStyle Or (lNewStyle And _
        WS_SYSMENU)
    lSavedStyle = lSavedStyle Or (lNewStyle And _
        WS_MINIMIZEBOX)
    lSavedStyle = lSavedStyle Or (lNewStyle And _
        WS_MAXIMIZEBOX)

    'remove the attributes for a dialog frame, a
    'ControlBox, a minimize button and a maximize button
    lNewStyle = lNewStyle And Not WS_DLGFRAME
    lNewStyle = lNewStyle And Not WS_SYSMENU
    lNewStyle = lNewStyle And Not WS_MINIMIZEBOX
    lNewStyle = lNewStyle And Not WS_MAXIMIZEBOX

    'is there a menu associated with this Form?
    iOldMenu = GetWindowWord%(frmIn.hWnd, GWW_ID)
    If iOldMenu <> 0 Then
        'yes-zero it the menu handle
        R = SetWindowWord%(frmIn.hWnd, GWW_ID, 0)
    End If
```

```
        'set the new style
        R = SetWindowLong&(frmIn.hWnd, GWL_STYLE, lNewStyle)

        'force Visual Basic to update the Form and get rid
    of the
        'title bar
        frmIn.Move frmIn.Left
        frmIn.Refresh
    End If
End Sub
```

Usage

To turn off the title bar, use:

```
ShowTitleBar Me, False
```

To turn it back on, use:

```
ShowTitleBar Me, True
```

Change A Form's Background Color To The Desktop Color

Compatible With   **Visual Basic 3.0, Visual Basic 4.0 16-bit**
Applies To   **Forms**

People have individual preferences when it comes to things like color. You can easily accommodate individual users' color preferences by using the GetSysColor API call. The following sample code shows how to retrieve the system's default background color. There are many other system colors you might like to know about. Here is a list of the Windows 3.1 system colors:

```
Global Const COLOR_SCROLLBAR = 0
Global Const COLOR_BACKGROUND = 1
Global Const COLOR_ACTIVECAPTION = 2
Global Const COLOR_INACTIVECAPTION = 3
Global Const COLOR_MENU = 4
Global Const COLOR_WINDOW = 5
Global Const COLOR_WINDOWFRAME = 6
```

```
Global Const COLOR_MENUTEXT = 7
Global Const COLOR_WINDOWTEXT = 8
Global Const COLOR_CAPTIONTEXT = 9
Global Const COLOR_ACTIVEBORDER = 10
Global Const COLOR_INACTIVEBORDER = 11
Global Const COLOR_APPWORKSPACE = 12
Global Const COLOR_HIGHLIGHT = 13
Global Const COLOR_HIGHLIGHTTEXT = 14
Global Const COLOR_BTNFACE = 15
Global Const COLOR_BTNSHADOW = 16
Global Const COLOR_GRAYTEXT = 17
Global Const COLOR_BTNTEXT = 18
Global Const COLOR_ENDCOLORS = COLOR_BTNTEXT
```

Declare The Following

```
Declare Function GetSysColor Lib "User" (ByVal nIndex%) _
    As Long
```

Code

```
Sub ColorFormBackground(frmForm as Form)
    Const COLOR_BACKGROUND = 1 'Desktop
    frmForm.BackColor = GetSysColor(COLOR_BACKGROUND)
End Sub
```

Usage

```
Private Sub Form_Load()
    ColorFormBackground Me
End Sub
```

Chapter 5 — Miscellaneous Tips

These are tips that did not seem to fall into any of the other categories. These include:

- Getting the number of instances of a running program

- Playing a WAV file from memory

Get The Number Of Instances Of A Running Program

Compatible With **Visual Basic 3.0, Visual Basic 4.0 16-bit**
Applies To **Applications**

There might be times when you want to prevent more than one instance of your program from running. The code below is a good example of how to do that by using API calls.

Declare The Following

```
Declare Function GetModuleHandle Lib "Kernel" _
    (ByVal FileName$) As Integer
Declare Function GetModuleUsage Lib "Kernel" _
    (ByVal hModule%) As Integer
Function Instances (sFileName As String) As Integer
    Instances = GetModuleUsage(GetModuleHandle(sFileName))
End Function
```

Example

```
Sub Form_Load ()
    Dim iNumInstances As Integer
    iNumInstances = Instances(CStr(App.EXEName))
    If iNumInstances > 1 Then
        End
    End If
End Sub
```

Error Handler

Compatible With   **Visual Basic 4.0**
Applies To   **Errors**

One of Visual Basic weak points has always been error handling. When an error happens, it usually brings down your program and possibly Windows too. To do effective error handling, you must write them into each and every routine. What a pain! There are many ways to do error handling, from coding it yourself to purchasing add-on tools that will do most of the code writing for you.

This tip is for those who prefer to do it themselves. This is a good idea, because you have much more control over it. Also, another important part of error handling is writing the error to a file. This will save you tons of time in development and also help with technical support problems. Instead of trying to get information on the error message from the user, they can simply send the error log. This tip incorporates that philosophy.

Declare The Following

```
Global Const errExit = 0
Global Const errResume = 1
Global Const errNext = 2
Global Const errSelect = 3
```

Code

```
Public Function ErrorHandler(iErrorNumber As Integer, _
        sErrText As String, iErrOption As Integer) _
        As Integer
    Dim sMessage As String
    Dim iReturn As Integer
```

```vb
            'Create message string
            sMessage = "Error #:" & Str(iErrorNumber) & " - "
            sMessage = sMessage & sErrText
            'Save to error log file
            ErrWriteLogFile sMessage

            Select Case iErrOption
                Case errExit
                    MsgBox sMessage, vbCritical, _
                        "Exiting program..."
                    GoTo errHandlerEnd
                Case errResume
                    MsgBox sMessage, vbCritical, "Error"
                    ErrorHandler = errResume
                Case errNext
                    MsgBox sMessage, vbCritical, "Error"
                    ErrorHandler = errNext
                Case errSelect
                    iReturn = MsgBox(sMessage, vbCritical + _
                        vbAbortRetryIgnore, "Error")
                    Select Case iReturn
                        Case Is = vbAbort
                            GoTo errHandlerEnd
                        Case Is = vbRetry
                            ErrorHandler = errResume
                        Case Is = vbIgnore
                            ErrorHandler = errNext
                    End Select
            End Select
        Exit Function
errHandlerEnd:
        MsgBox "Click OK to Exit Program"
        End
End Function

Public Sub ErrWriteLogFile(sLogMsg As String)
        Dim sFile As String
        Dim lFile As Long
        Dim sErrDir As String
```

```
    On Error GoTo errWriteLogFileErr
    sErrDir = App.Path
    lFile = FreeFile
    sFile = sErrDir & "\" & App.EXEName & ".err"
    Open sFile For Append As lFile
    Print #lFile, Format$(Now, "General Date") & ": " _
        & sLogMsg
    Close #lFile
    GoTo errWriteLogFileExit
errWriteLogFileErr:
    MsgBox Str(Err) + "-" + Error$, vbCritical, _
        "Unable to Write Error Log"
    Exit Sub
errWriteLogFileExit:
End Sub
```

Example

This is a sample of how you could use this tip:

```
Dim R As Long
Dim I As Integer
On Error GoTo ErrorHandler1
    For I = 3000 To 100000
        DoEvents
    Next I
ErrorHandler1:
    R = ErrorHandler(iErrorNumber:=Err.Number,
    sErrText:=Err.Description, iErrOption:=errNext)
```

Even though this tip was written in Visual Basic 4.0, it can be easily modified for any other version of Visual Basic. It's also easy to modify for your particular needs.

Extracting An Icon From A Program

Compatible With   Visual Basic 3.0
Applies To   Icons

Did you ever want to display an icon from an external program for users to click on? Well, it's simple with the following code:

Declare The Following

```
Declare Function ExtractIcon Lib "Shell" (ByVal hInstance _
    As Integer, ByVal pszExeName As String, ByVal iIcon _
    As Integer) As Integer
Declare Function DrawIcon Lib "User" (ByVal hDC As _
    Integer, ByVal X As Integer, ByVal Y As Integer, _
    ByVal hIcon As Integer) As Integer
```

Code

```
Sub SetupIcon (sEXEFileName As String, iIconNum As _
        Integer, picPictureBox As PictureBox)
    Dim iIcon As Integer

    iIcon = ExtractIcon(0, sEXEFileName, iIconNum)
    picPictureBox.Tag = CStr(iIcon)
End Sub
```

This routine gets the integer handle to the icon and stores it in the Picture Box's Tag property for use during painting.

```
Sub PaintIcon (picPictureBox As PictureBox)
    Dim X As Integer

    If Len(picPictureBox.Tag) > 0 Then
        X = DrawIcon(picPictureBox.hDC, 0, 0, _
            CInt(picPictureBox.Tag))
    End If
End Sub
```

Every time the PictureBox is notified by Windows to Paint, this routine uses the icon handle storied in the Tag property and draws it into the picture box.

Example

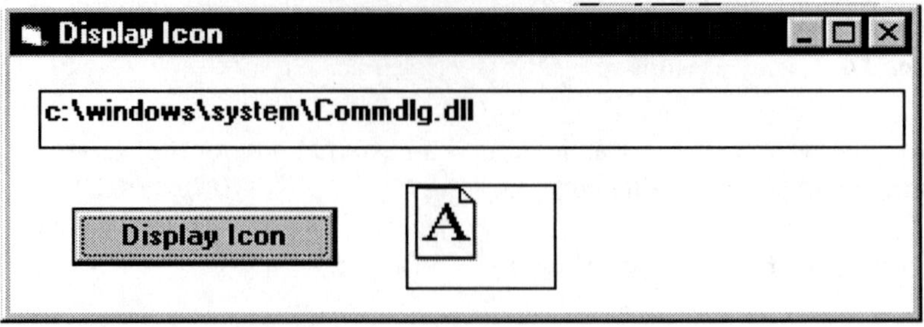

```
Sub Command1_Click ()
    SetupIcon CStr(text1.Text), 0, Picture1
    Picture1_Paint
End Sub


Sub Picture1_Paint ()
    PaintIcon Picture1
End Sub
```

This code will work on EXE, VBX, OCX and DLL files.

Launching The 32-bit MSInfo Program

Compatible With   **Visual Basic 4.0 32-bit**
Applies To   **MSInfo**

Ever try to ask a user for specific information about their operating system? Things like, what version of Windows 95 are they using, how much memory is installed, and so on? Microsoft has included a program called Microsoft System Information with Windows 95 and Windows NT 4.0. This program tells you everything about the system! To call it, use the following code.

Declare

```
Private Declare Function RegOpenKeyEx Lib _
    "advapi32.dll" Alias "RegOpenKeyExA" (ByVal hKey _
    As Long, ByVal lpSubKey As String, ByVal ulOptions _
    As Long, ByVal samDesired As Long, phkResult As Long) _
    As Long
Private Declare Function RegQueryValueEx Lib _
```

```vb
        "advapi32.dll" Alias "RegQueryValueExA" (ByVal hKey _
    As Long, ByVal lpValueName As String, ByVal _
    lpReserved As Long, lpType As Long, ByVal lpData _
    As String, lpcbData As Long) As Long
Private Declare Function RegCloseKey Lib "advapi32.dll" _
    (ByVal hKey As Long) As Long
Private Const HKEY_LOCAL_MACHINE = &H80000002
Private Const ERROR_SUCCESS = 0&
Private Const READ_CONTROL = &H20000
Private Const KEY_NOTIFY = &H10
Private Const KEY_ENUMERATE_SUB_KEYS = &H8
Private Const KEY_QUERY_VALUE = &H1
Private Const SYNCHRONIZE = &H100000
Private Const STANDARD_RIGHTS_READ = (READ_CONTROL)
Private Const KEY_READ = ((STANDARD_RIGHTS_READ Or _
    KEY_QUERY_VALUE Or KEY_ENUMERATE_SUB_KEYS Or _
    KEY_NOTIFY) And (Not SYNCHRONIZE))
Public gsSysInfoPath As String
```

Code

```vb
Public Sub SetSysInfo()
    Dim lRetVal As Long
    Dim sTemp As String
    Dim lNewKey As Long
    Dim lValType As Long
    Dim lKeySize As Long

    sTemp = Space(255)

    lRetVal = RegOpenKeyEx(HKEY_LOCAL_MACHINE, _
        "software\microsoft\shared tools\msinfo", _
        0, KEY_READ, lNewKey)

    If lRetVal = ERROR_SUCCESS Then
        lKeySize = LenB(sTemp)
        lRetVal = RegQueryValueEx(lNewKey, "Path", _
            0, lValType, sTemp, lKeySize)

        If lRetVal = ERROR_SUCCESS Then
            gsSysInfoPath = Left$(sTemp, lKeySize)
```

```
        End If
    End If

    lRetVal = RegCloseKey(lNewKey)
End Sub
```

Example

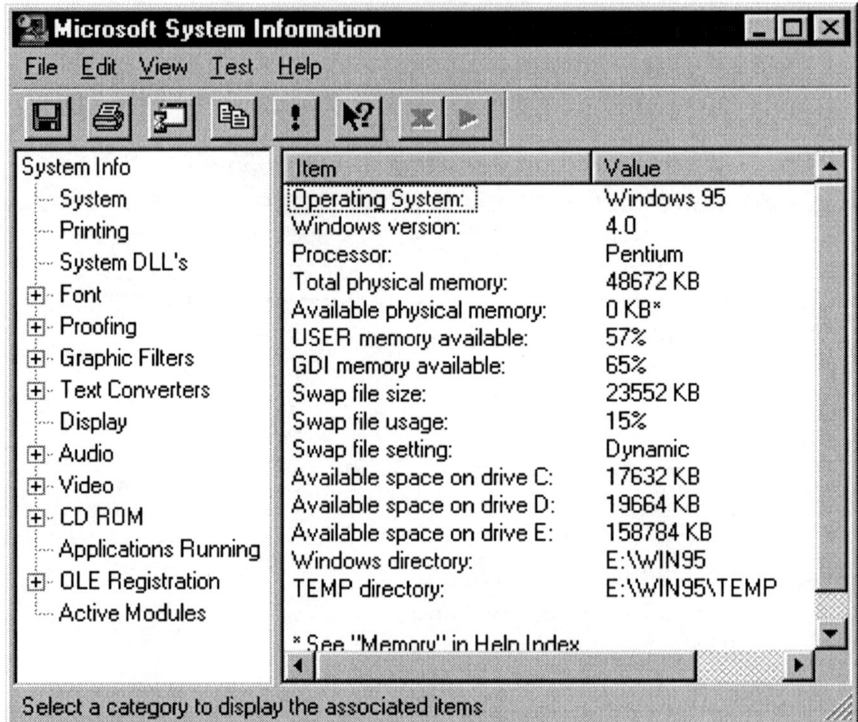

During Form_Load, call SetSysInfo to find out where the program is located.

```
Private Sub Form_Load()
    SetSysInfo
End Sub
```

This puts the information into the gsSysInfoPath variable. Then, when the program is needed, use this code:

```
Dim lRetVal As Long
lRetVal = Shell(gsSysInfoPath, vbNormalFocus)
```

Loading And Playing A WAV From Memory

Compatible With   **Visual Basic 3.0, Visual Basic 4.0 16-bit**
Applies To   **Wave Files**

Did you ever want to load a WAV file into memory and keep it there and play it from your program? Why would you want to do this? If you have a screen saver, game or multi-media program that uses one or more sounds consistently through your program, by loading it into memory, it will keep the disk hits down and allow them to play quicker.

It's simple and straight-forward. Just load the file into memory (a string) and use the following API command to play it:

```
sndPlaySound(WaveDataBuffer$, SND_ASYN_NODEF_MEMORY)
```

Declare The Following

```
Declare Function sndPlaySound Lib "MMSYSTEM.DLL" (ByVal _
    WaveFile As Any, ByVal wFlags%) As Integer
Declare Function lopen Lib "Kernel" Alias "_lopen" _
    (ByVal lpPathName As String, ByVal iReadWrite _
    As Integer) As Integer
Declare Function lclose Lib "Kernel" Alias "_lclose" _
    (ByVal hFile As Integer) As Integer
Declare Function lread Lib "Kernel" Alias "_lread" _
    (ByVal hFile As Integer, ByVal lpBuffer As String, _
    ByVal wBytes As Integer) As Integer
Global Const SND_ASYN = &H1
Global Const SND_NODEFAULT = &H2
Global Const SND_MEM = &H4
Global Const SND_Asyn_Nodef_Memory = (SND_ASYN + _
    SND_NODEFAULT + SND_MEM)
Global Const SND_HasFinished = &H10
Global Const MB_ICONSTOP = 16
Global gsWaveDataBuffer As String
Global giWaveFileHandle As Integer
Global giWaveFileName as Integer
```

Code

Load the file into memory.

```
Function LoadFileToMemory (sFileName As String) As Integer
    'return code (integer)
    Dim R As Integer

    'Check out space required to hold file data:
    'If size exceeds boundary of Visual Basic "integer" data
    type
    '(32768 bytes) we shouldn't try to proceed, because
    'lread uses integer variable as "size of buffer"
    If FileLen(sFileName) > 32767 Then
        MsgBox "File is too large - can't load." _
            & Chr$(10) & "(Max. file size 32,767 bytes)", _
            MB_ICONSTOP, "Sorry, but..."
        LoadFileToMemory = False
        Exit Function
    End If

    'Allocate buffer
    gsWaveDataBuffer = Space$(FileLen(sFileName))

    'Open file - this will return the file handle
    'flag value "0": open for read-only
    giWaveFileHandle = lopen(sFileName, 0)

    'read data into buffer.
    R = lread(giWaveFileHandle, gsWaveDataBuffer,
    FileLen(sFileName))

    'close the file.
    R = lclose(giWaveFileHandle)

    LoadFileToMemory = True
End Function
```

Play the file.

```
Dim R As Integer
R = sndPlaySound(gsWaveDataBuffer, SND_Asyn_Nodef_Memory)
```

It's important to make sure your wave file is done playing before the program ends. Use the following code in the QueryUnload event.

```
Sub Form_QueryUnload (Cancel As Integer, UnloadMode _
        As Integer)
    Dim R as Integer

    R = 0
    form1.MousePointer = 11
    'As long as a sound is playing... do events
    Do While R = 0
        R = sndPlaySound("", SND_HasFinished)
        DoEvents
    Loop

    form1.MousePointer = 0
End Sub
```

Reading And Writing INI Files

Compatible With   **Visual Basic 3.0**
Applies To   **INI Files**

Most programs need to keep some sort of settings information. This is commonly used for setting up file paths, registration numbers, the form's last location, users' names and tons of varying but specific information. You could keep this in your own file format, but Windows has given us a simpler way to do this by using initialization (INI) files.

Not only are INI files easy to use, but they are fast! Even though Microsoft wants us to use the registration database for this type of information in Visual Basic 4.0 and Visual Basic 5.0, INI files are still faster and the only way to keep this type of informaion local to your program. This way, if the Registration Database gets wiped out or corrupted, your program will still work.

Using INI files is not built into Visual Basic 3.0 and below. To further complicate matters, Microsoft has not done a good job of documenting INI file use for Visual Basic programmers.

In this tip, we will go over the major functions you can do with an INI file.

Declare The Following

```
Declare Function WritePrivateProfileString Lib "Kernel" _
    (ByVal AppName As String, ByVal KeyName As String, _
    ByVal NewString As String, ByVal filename As String) _
    As Integer
Declare Function GetPrivateProfileString Lib "Kernel" _
    (ByVal AppName As String, ByVal KeyName As String, _
    ByVal default As String, ByVal ReturnedString As _
    String, ByVal MAXSIZE As Integer, ByVal filename As _
    String) As Integer
Declare Function GetProfileInt Lib "Kernel" (ByVal _
    lpAppName As String, ByVal lpKeyName As String, _
    ByVal nDefault As String) As Integer
Declare Function GetProfileString Lib "Kernel" (ByVal _
    lpAppName As String, ByVal lpKeyName As String, _
    ByVal lpDefault As String, ByVal lpReturnedString _
    As String, ByVal nSize As Integer) As Integer
Declare Function WriteProfileString Lib "Kernel" _
    (ByVal lpAppName As String, ByVal lpKeyName As _
    String, ByVal lpString As String) As Integer
Declare Function GetPrivateProfileInt Lib "Kernel" _
    (ByVal lpAppName As String, ByVal lpKeyName As _
    String, ByVal nDefault As Integer, ByVal lpFileName _
    As String) As Integer
```

You will notice here that there are basically two different types of INI files, private and non-private. Private profile calls should be used for your program's INI file while the non-private profile calls should be used for the WIN.INI file that's found in the C:\WINDOWS directory..

Parameter Values

Here is some terminology you will need to remember when dealing with INI files.

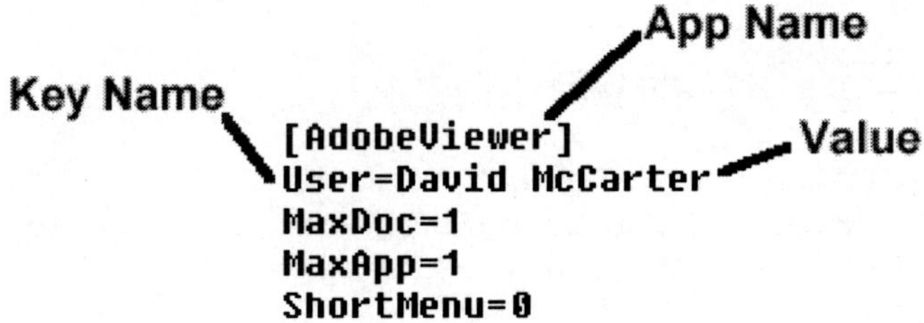

AppName: Heading of the section in an INI file.

KeyName: Key within a heading.

Value: Value either being set or retrieved.

Reading An INI File

For most purposes, you will be reading either strings or integers from INI files. Well, for that matter, everything could be strings and you can convert them to integers.

Reading Integer Values

```
Function iReadINI (sAppName As String, sKeyName As _
      String, sFilename As String, iDefault As Integer) _
      As Integer

   iReadINI = GetPrivateProfileInt(sAppName, _
      ByVal sKeyName, iDefault, sFilename)
End Function
```

Usage

```
Dim iMyValue As Integer
iMyValue = GetPrivateProfileInt("VBTT", "Download", _
   App.Path & "\VBTT.INI", 0)
```

One key thing to remember, here when writing or reading INI files, is that if you don't specifically specify a path where for the INI file. Windows, by default, puts it in the C:\WINDOWS directory. In most cases, you would want to keep your INI file in the same directory as your application. It makes it easier to remove all traces of your program, if needed.

Reading String Values

```
Function sReadINI (sAppName As String, sKeyName As _
        String, sFilename As String) As String
    Dim sReturn As String

    sReturn = String(255, Chr(0))

    sReadINI = Left(sReturn,
    GetPrivateProfileString(sAppName, ByVal sKeyName, "",
    sReturn, Len(sReturn), sFilename))
End Function
```

Since this API call returns a string, we need to first create a string large enough to hold the return value. Since most of the time, that length is unknown, it's better to create a large string. That's why this code uses the maximum of 255 characters.

You can change the code to return a default value, but, in my experience, I have not found a use for it. If there is no value, then it's never been set.

Usage

```
Dim sMyValue As String
sMyValue = sReadINI("VBTT", "Download Directory", _
    App.Path & "\VBTT.INI")
```

Note

One thing to remember about when reading reading INI files: if the INI file does not exist you will get an empty string, when reading strings, or the default value, when reading integers.

Writing To An INI File

Writing to an INI file is just as easy. I always use the WriteProfileString, because any value can be sent, including integers.

Code

```
Sub WriteINI (sAppName As String, sKeyName As String, _
        sNewString As String, sFilename As String)
    Dim R As Integer

    R = WritePrivateProfileString(sAppName, sKeyName, _
        sNewString, sFilename)
```

```
End Sub
```

Usage

```
WriteINI "VBTT", "Download Directory", _
    "c:\Vbtt\download", App.Path & "\VBTT.INI"
```

Removing KeyNames And AppNames Sections

Now for some tricks that are very hard to find. How about if you want to remove a Key or AppName? Well, it's straight-forward too, just not well documented.

Declare The Following

```
Declare Function RemovePrivateProfileString Lib _
    "Kernel" Alias "WritePrivateProfileString" (ByVal _
    AppName As String, ByVal KeyName As Any, ByVal _
    NewString As Any, ByVal filename As String) As Integer
```

Here we are using the Alias feature of an API call. We are just renaming the WritePrivateProfileString call to a new name of RemovePrivateProfileString. This way, we can pass it a key "As Any". We are doing this because the value that we will use is not a string, but we want to keep the "As String" in the original WritePrivateProfileString call for type checking.

Removing KeyNamess

```
Sub RemoveKeyName (sAppName As String, sKey As String, _
        sFileName As String)
    Dim R As Integer

    R = RemovePrivateProfileString(sAppName, sKey, 0&, _
        sFileName)
End Sub
```

Usage

```
RemoveKeyName "VBTT", "Download Directory", _
    App.Path & "\VBTT.INI"
```

The trick here is the 0&, in the place the value would normally be used, will erase the key from the INI file.

Removing AppName Section

```
Sub RemoveAppNameSection (sAppName As String, _
        sFileName As String)
    Dim R As Integer

    R = RemovePrivateProfileString(sAppName, 0&, 0&, _
        sFileName)
End Sub
```

Usage

```
RemoveAppNameSection "VBTT", App.Path & "\VBTT.INI"
```

There you have the most commonly used API calls for reading and writing INI files.

Reading And Writing Screen Saver Passwords

Compatible With   **Visual Basic 3.0, Visual Basic 4.0 16-bit**
Applies To   **Screen Savers**

During a beta test of one of my screen savers, a beta tester pointed out that I was using my own password protection scheme. My method differs from the scheme used in the screen savers that come with Windows. That beta tester wanted me to use the same password as the Windows screen savers. This is a great idea. This means that the user does not have to remember two different passwords.

After some digging, I found some C code that handled the encryption. Here's a Visual Basic version of it!

How To Use The Code

To check to see if the user entered the same password that's in the CONTROL.INI file, just call the EncryptPassWord function:

```
If EncryptPassWord(txtPassWord(0).Text) = _
        sGetPassWord() Then
    'Your Code Goes Here
End If
```

To write a new password into CONTROL.INI, just call the SavePassWord function:

```
Call SavePassWord(EncryptPassWord(txtPassWord(2).Text))
```

Declare

```
Declare Function WritePrivateProfileString Lib "Kernel" _
    (ByVal AppName As String, ByVal KeyName As String, _
    ByVal NewString As String, ByVal filename As String) _
    As Integer
Declare Function GetPrivateProfileString Lib "Kernel" _
    (ByVal AppName As String, ByVal KeyName As String, _
    ByVal default As String, ByVal ReturnedString As _
    String, ByVal MAXSIZE As Integer, ByVal filename _
    As String) As Integer
```

Code

```
Function sGetPassWord () As String
    Dim sTempPass As String

    sTempPass = sReadINI("ScreenSaver", "Password", _
        "control.ini")
    sGetPassWord = sTempPass
End Function

Sub SavePassWord (sPassWord As String)
    Dim R As Integer

    Call WriteINI("ScreenSaver", "Password", sPassWord, _
        "control.ini")
End Sub

Function sEncryptPassWord (ByVal sArg As String) As String
    Dim iArgPt As Integer
    Dim iArgChar As Integer
    Dim iArgLen As Integer

    iArgLen = Len(sArg)

    If iArgLen = 0 Then
        Exit Function' Nothing to check
```

```
        End If

        sArg = UCase$(sArg)

        'First Pass
        For iArgPt = 1 To iArgLen
            iArgChar = Asc(Mid$(sArg, iArgPt, 1))
            Call PassXor(iArgLen, iArgChar)
            If iArgPt = 1 Then
                Call PassXor(42, iArgChar)
            Else
                Call PassXor(iArgPt - 1, iArgChar)
                Call PassXor(Asc(Mid$(sArg, iArgPt - 1)), _
                    iArgChar)
            End If

            Mid$(sArg, iArgPt, 1) = Chr$(iArgChar)
        Next iArtPt

        'Second Pass
        If iArgLen > 1 Then
            For iArgPt = iArgLen To 1 Step -1
                iArgChar = Asc(Mid$(sArg, iArgPt, 1))
                Call PassXor(iArgLen, iArgChar)

                If iArgPt = iArgLen Then
                    Call PassXor(42, iArgChar)
                Else
                    Call PassXor(iArgPt - 1, iArgChar)
                    Call PassXor(Asc(Mid$(sArg, iArgPt + 1, _
                        1)), iArgChar)
                End If
                Mid$(sArg, iArgPt, 1) = Chr$(iArgChar)
            Next iArtPt
        End If

        sEncryptPassWord = sArg
End Function

Sub PassXor (x1 As Integer, x2 As Integer)
    Select Case x2 Xor x1
```

```
            Case 0 To 32, 127 To 144, 147 To 159, 61, 91, 93
                ' not allowed
            Case Else
                x2 = x2 Xor x1
        End Select
End Sub


Function sReadINI (sAppName As String, sKeyName As String, _
        sFilename As String) As String
    Dim sReturn As String

    sReturn = String(255, Chr(0))

    sReadINI = Left(sReturn, _
        GetPrivateProfileString(sAppName, ByVal sKeyName, _
        "", sReturn, Len(sReturn), sFilename))
End Function


Sub WriteINI (sAppName As String, sKeyName As _
        String, sNewString As String, sFilename As String)
    Dim R As Integer

    R = WritePrivateProfileString(sAppName, _
        sKeyName, sNewString, sFilename)
End Sub
```

Chapter 6 — API World

For the most part, these tips deal with Windows API calls. If you are new to Visual Basic, you will soon find out that you need to extend the capabilities of the programming language. Calling Windows APIs directly is a great way to add extra functionality to your programs.

There are hundreds of API calls built into Windows! Most of them you can use directly from Visual Basic. So you can do just about anything a C programmer can do.

Some of the API calls discussed in this chapter are:

- Checking for a DOS window

- Dragging a Form or Control

- Hiding a DOS Window's Icon

- Hiding the cursor

- Using a Windows 95 directory dialog box

- Easy About Box

Checking For A DOS Window

Compatible With   **Visual Basic 3.0, Visual Basic 4.0 16-bit**
Applies To   **Window**

There are times when you might need to know if a window is a DOS window and all you have is the window handle. To find out if a window is a DOS window you only need to do the following two things:

Get the task handle for your window handle with the "GetWindowTask" API call.

Test this "IsWinOldApTask" API call for true.

The following declare statement outlines the IsDOSWindow API call:

```
Declare Function IsWinOldApTask% Lib "kernel" Alias _
    "#158" (ByVal hTask%)
```

In the "kernel" (ex: KRNL386.EXE) file, the exported function, "158", points to this routine. Although undocumented, this API call was supported internally in Windows 3.0 and continues to thrive in the 3.1 and 3.11 versions. It probably won't be around for future Windows versions as DOS seems to be on the way out.

The following example code makes use of this rare API call.

Declare The Following

```
Declare Function IsWinOldApTask% Lib "kernel" _
    Alias "#158" (ByVal hTask%)
Declare Function GetWindowTask% Lib "user" (ByVal hWnd%)
Declare Function FindWindow% Lib "user" (ByVal ClassName$,
    ByVal lpWindowName As Any)

Function IsDOSWindow (iHandle As Integer) As Long
    IsDOSWindow = IsWinOldApTask (GetWindowTask (iHandle))
End Function
```

Example

```
Dim iInstance As Integer
Dim iFoundWindow As Integer

'launch a DOS window
iInstance = Shell ("COMMAND.COM", 1)
'Get the window handle
iFoundWindow = FindWindow ("tty", 0&)
If IsDOSWindow (iFoundWindow) = True Then
    MsgBox "YES, it IS a DOS window"
End If
```

Compacting Memory

Compatible With   **Visual Basic 3.0, Visual Basic 4.0 16-bit**
Applies To   **Windows 3**

You may sometimes find yourself writing an application that uses a lot of memory. A multimedia screen saver with animation and sound is a perfect example of such an application. If a user's system's memory is fragmented, the screen saver will run very slowly, or it might not start at all. You can use the following function to defragment memory, making the maximum available to your program, before beginning any operation that will require a lot of memory.

Declare

```
Declare Function GlobalCompact Lib "Kernel" _
    (ByVal dwMinFree&) As Long
```

Code

```
Sub CompactMemory ()
    Dim R As Long

    R = GlobalCompact(&HFFFFFFFF)
End Sub
```

Usage

```
Call CompatMemory
```

Determine The Number Of Colors Available

Compatible With   **Visual Basic 3.0, Visual Basic 4.0 16-bit**
Applies To   **Windows 3 and Windows 95**

Sometimes you really need to know how many colors a user's system supports. The following function uses the GetDeviceCaps API call to retrieve that information from the system.

Declare

```
Declare Function GetDC Lib "User" (ByVal hWnd%) As Integer
Declare Function ReleaseDC Lib "User" (ByVal hWnd%, _
    ByVal hDC%) As Integer
Declare Function GetDesktopWindow Lib "User" () As Integer
```

Code

```
Function dGetSysColors () As Double
    Dim R As Integer
    Const BITSPIXEL = 12
    Const PLANES = 14
    Dim hSrcDC As Integer

    hSrcDC = GetDC(GetDesktopWindow())
    dGetSysColors = GetDeviceCaps(hSrcDC, PLANES) * 2 ^
    GetDeviceCaps(hSrcDC, BITSPIXEL)
    R = ReleaseDC(GetDesktopWindow(), hSrcDC)
End Function
```

Usage

```
Dim dSysColors As Double
sSysColors = dGetSysColors()
```

Hiding A DOS Window And Icon

Compatible With   **Visual Basic 3.0, Visual Basic 4.0 16-bit**
Applies To   **Window**

To hide a DOS Window or Icon, try using an API called WinExec with nCmdShow set to SW_HIDE to hide the DOS window.

Declare The Following

```
Declare Function WinExec Lib "Kernel" (ByVal lpCmdLine _
    As String, ByVal nCmdShow As Integer) As Integer
Declare Function GetModuleUsage Lib "Kernel" (ByVal _
    hModule As Integer) As Integer
Global Const SW_HIDE = 0
Global Const SW_NORMAL = 1
Global Const SW_MAXIMIZE = 3
Global Const SW_MINIMIZE = 6
```

Usage

```
R = WinExec("dosprmpt.pif /c YOUR DOS COMMAND HERE", _
    SW_HIDE)

Do While GetModuleUsage(R) > 0
    DoEvents
Loop
```

To use this technique, you must have the DOSPRMPT.PIF set to run in windowed mode (use the PIF editor). The while loop will wait until the WinExec SHELL is done before exiting. Leave it out if you don't have to wait for the SHELL to complete before going on with the program.

Dragging A Form Or Control

Compatible With   **Visual Basic 3.0, Visual Basic 4.0 16-bit**
Applies To   **Form, Controls**

Here's an easy way to let users move forms or controls around at runtime. Unlike other techniques that require capturing the mouse, moving the control or form as the mouse moves, and releasing the mouse when its button is no longer pressed, this technique requires only two simple API calls.

Declare The Following

```
Declare Sub ReleaseCapture Lib "User" ()
Declare Sub SendMessage Lib "User" (ByVal hWnd As _
     Integer, ByVal wMsg As Integer, ByVal wParam As _
     Integer, lParam As Long)
Const WM_SYSCOMMAND = &H112
Const SC_MOVE = &HF012
```

Code

Put the following lines in the MouseDown procedure of whatever form or control you want to allow the user to drag:

```
ReleaseCapture
SendMessage Thing.hWnd, WM_SYSCOMMAND, SC_MOVE, 0
```

Hiding The Cursor

Compatible With   **Visual Basic 3.0, Visual Basic 4.0 16-bit**
Applies To   **Cursor**

From time to time, you might have the need to hide the cursor from the user. This could be used in multi-media applications and screen savers. You could move the cursor off the screen, but there is an easy way to make the cursor invisible with an API call:

Declare The Following

```
Declare Function ShowCursor Lib "User" (ByVal bShow _
     As Integer) As Integer
```

Usage

To use the API, simply call:

```
R = ShowCursor(True)
```

or

```
R = ShowCursor(False)
```

There is one thing you should know about this API call. Whenever a program calls ShowCursor, Windows keeps an internal count of how many times ShowCursor was called. The problem is that there is no way to retrieve this counter. So just calling ShowCursor(False) might not work because it just decreases the counter by one. Unless the counter is zero, the cursor will not disappear. Use this routine instead.

```
Sub EnableCursor (iSetting As Integer)
    Select Case iSetting
        Case True
            Do While ShowCursor(True) <= 0
            Loop
        Case False
            Do While ShowCursor(False) >= 0
            Loop
    End Select
End Sub
```

To use this Sub, call it with the iSetting parameter set to either True or False. The cool thing about this API call is that it makes the cursor invisible but MouseMove, etc., events still work. This technique also works in Windows 95.

Making Text Boxes Read Only

Compatible With	**Visual Basic 3.0, Visual Basic 4.0 16-bit**
Applies To	**Text Box**

Here is how to make a Text Box read only and prevent the user from changing the text. There are a number of ways to approach this problem. For instance, you can grab either the KeyPress or KeyDown events and set the KeyAscii parameter to zero. However, the best idea is to use the Windows API SendMessage function to tell the control to become read-only.

Declare The Following

```
Global Const WM_USER = &H400
Global Const EM_SETREADONLY = (WM_USER + 31)
Declare Function SendMessage Lib "User" (ByVal hWnd As _
    Integer, ByVal wMsg As Integer, ByVal wParam As _
    Integer, lParam As Any) As Long
```

Usage

```
Dim R As Integer
R = SendMessage(Text1.hWnd, EM_SETREADONLY, 1, 0)
```

Prompting The User For A Directory In Win95

Compatible With   **Visual Basic 4.0 32-bit**
Applies To   **Windows 95**

Windows common dialogs are great if you want the user to select a file, but what if you want the user to select a directory? Call the following function, BrowseForFolder, which relies on Win32's new SHBrowseForFolder function:

Declare The Following

```
Private Type BrowseInfo
    hWndOwner As Long
    pIDLRoot As Long
    pszDisplayName As Long
    lpszTitle As Long
    ulFlags As Long
    lpfnCallback As Long
    lParam As Long
    iImage As Long
End Type
Private Const BIF_RETURNONLYFSDIRS = 1
Private Const MAX_PATH = 260

Private Declare Sub CoTaskMemFree Lib "ole32.dll" _
    (ByVal hMem As Long)
Private Declare Function lstrcat Lib "kernel32" Alias _
    "lstrcatA" (ByVal lpString1 As String, ByVal _
    lpString2 As String) As Long
Private Declare Function SHBrowseForFolder Lib "shell32" _
    (lpbi As BrowseInfo) As Long
Private Declare Function SHGetPathFromIDList Lib "shell32" _
    (ByVal pidList As Long, ByVal lpBuffer As String) _
    As Long
```

Code

```
Public Function BrowseForFolder(hWndOwner As Long, _
        sPrompt As String) As String
    Dim iNull As Integer
    Dim lpIDList As Long
    Dim lResult As Long
```

```vb
    Dim sPath As String
    Dim udtBI As BrowseInfo

    With udtBI
        .hWndOwner = hWndOwner
        .lpszTitle = lstrcat(sPrompt, "")
        .ulFlags = BIF_RETURNONLYFSDIRS
    End With


    lpIDList = SHBrowseForFolder(udtBI)
    If lpIDList Then
        sPath = String$(MAX_PATH, 0)
        lResult = SHGetPathFromIDList(lpIDList, sPath)
        Call CoTaskMemFree(lpIDList)
        iNull = InStr(sPath, vbNullChar)
        If iNull Then
            sPath = Left$(sPath, iNull - 1)
        End If
    End If
    BrowseForFolder = sPath
End Function
```

Usage

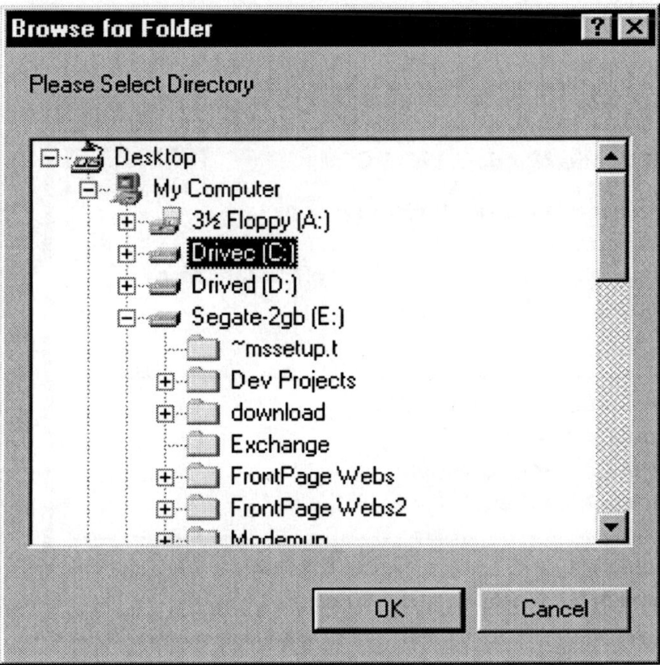


```
sDirectoryName = BrowseForFolder(Me.hWnd, _
    "Please Select Directory")
```

Quick And Easy About Box

Compatible With   Visual Basic 3.0, Visual Basic 4.0 16-bit

Most programs need an About Box. Did you know that there is an easy way to make one
with only two lines of code? You simply use the ShellAbout API call in the SHELL.DLL
file.

Declare The Following

```
Declare Sub ShellAbout Lib "shell.dll" (ByVal hWndOwner _
    As Integer, ByVal lpszAppName As String, ByVal _
    lpszMoreInfo As String, ByVal hIcon As Integer)
```

Usage

```
Call ShellAbout(Me.hWnd, app.Title, _
     "Copyright 1995, My Company", Me.Icon)
```

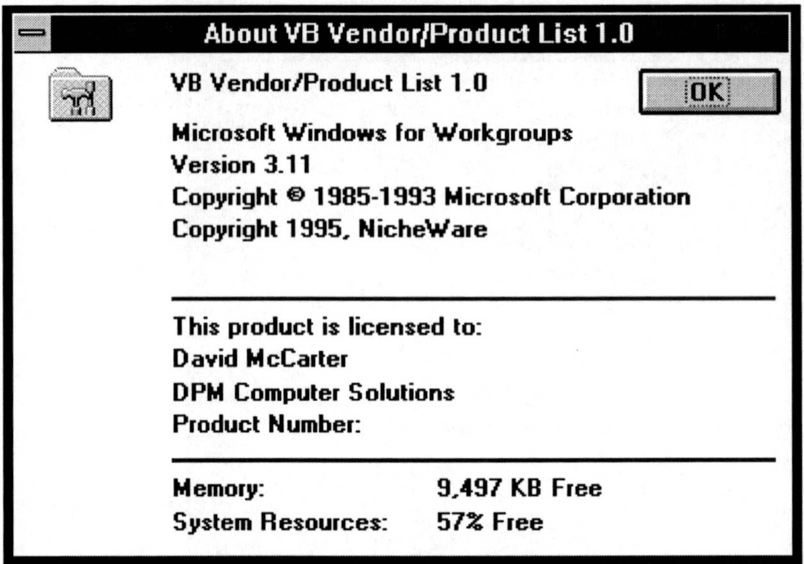

The first parameter is the handle to the Form that is calling the About Box. The second is the caption. In this example we simply used the App.Title call to insert the application name from the EXE. The third is for extra information. It's a good idea to put copyright information here. The last parameter is the handle to the icon you wish to be displayed in the upper left corner.

Setting Program Focus

Compatible With   **Visual Basic 3.0, Visual Basic 4.0 16-bit**
Applies To   **Window**

Sometimes it may be useful to inhibit the user from switching to other programs than yours, or to disable Windows standard sequences such as ALT+ TAB or CTRL + ESCAPE. This may be very useful, for instance, when the user is a novice and for some reason he must not leave the application until he closes it down. To test this example, insert the following line of code in the declaration section of a generic Form1 module.

Declare The Following

```
Declare Function SetSysModalWindow Lib "User" (ByVal _
    hWnd As Integer) As Integer
```

Code

Then insert the following line of code in the Load event of the Form:

```
i% = SetSysModalWindow (form1.hwnd)
```

When the user closes the application, normal Windows functionality is automatically restored.

Use this API call wisely. You are locking your users from accessing any other window. If your program errors out, you could lock up your user's computer if your program does not end properly.

Waiting For A Shelled Program To End

Compatible With   **All Versions of Visual Basic**
Applies To   **Shell**

There are many times that you might want to start an external program and wait for it to end before your application continues. Using the Shell method, in any version of Visual Basic, does not allow you to do this. You will need to use an API call and wait for the called program to end. We will discuss how to do this in 16-bit versions of Visual Basic and 32-bit versions.

Shelling From Visual Basic 16-bit.

This code will work under any 16-bit version of Visual Basic. Waiting for a program to end is simple.

Declare

```
Declare Function GetModuleUsage Lib "Kernel" (ByVal _
    hModule As Integer) As Integer
Declare Function WinExec Lib "Kernel" (ByVal lpCmdLine _
    As String, ByVal nCmdShow As Integer) As Integer

Global Const SW_HIDE = 0
```

```
Global Const SW_SHOWNORMAL = 1
Global Const SW_NORMAL = 1
Global Const SW_SHOWMINIMIZED = 2
Global Const SW_SHOWMAXIMIZED = 3
Global Const SW_MAXIMIZE = 3
Global Const SW_SHOWNOACTIVATE = 4
Global Const SW_SHOW = 5
Global Const SW_MINIMIZE = 6
Global Const SW_SHOWMINNOACTIVE = 7
Global Const SW_SHOWNA = 8
Global Const SW_RESTORE = 9
```

Code

```
Sub DoShell (sShellString As String, iWinType As Integer)
    Dim iInstanceHandle As Integer
    Dim X As Integer

    iInstanceHandle = WinExec(sShellString, iWinType)

    Do While GetModuleUsage(iInstanceHandle) > 0
        X = DoEvents()
    Loop
End Sub
```

Usage

```
DoShell "C:\DOS\FORMAT.COM", SW_HIDE
```

This code uses the WinExec API call to start the program and return the instance handle. We simply sit in a DoEvents loop until GetModuleUsage (using the instance handle as the parameter) tells us that the instance of that called program is gone. You also can start the program in any of the SW_ modes you like, including hiding it!

Shelling From Visual Basic 32-bit.

Shelling from a 16-bit version of Visual Basic is easy. Things are not so easy in 32-bit environments. With Windows 95 or Windows NT, every program runs its own distinct environment, which precludes polling if an instance of a program still exists. The following code will do the trick.

Declare

```
Declare Function OpenProcess Lib "kernel32" (ByVal _
    dwDesiredaccess&, ByVal bInherithandle&, _
    ByVal dwProcessid&) As Long
Declare Function GetExitCodeProcess Lib "kernel32" _
    (ByVal hProcess As Long, lpexitcode As Long) As Long
Const STILL_ACTIVE = &H103
Const PROCESS_QUERY_INFORMATION = &H400
```

Code

```
Sub ShellWait(sCommandLine As String)
    Dim hShell As Long
    Dim hProc As Long
    Dim lExit As Long

    hShell = Shell(sCommandLine, vbNormalFocus)
    hProc = OpenProcess(PROCESS_QUERY_INFORMATION, _
        False, hShell)
    Do
        GetExitCodeProcess hProc, lExit
        DoEvents
    Loop While lExit = STILL_ACTIVE
End Sub
```

Usage

```
ShellWait sCommandLine:="notepad.exe"
```

The trick with this code, as opposed to the method that the Microsoft KnowledgeBase has, is that it Shells the required program and then opens a process. It then waits for that process to finish. This way, if the program you Shelled calls other programs, you can continue on after the main (parent) program closes.

For example, if you Shelled the Internet Explorer, and the user started a download, you would not be able to continue until that download is done, even if the user closed Explorer. There might be times when you require this behavior (refer to article Q96844 of the Visual Basic KnowledgeBase). That code gives you an alternative.

Chapter 7 — Speed And Size Tips

These tips are good ones to speed up your program. Most of the tips in this chapter are what most seasoned programmers already know. Using the tips and tricks in this chapter, you will be able to program like a pro in no time! Some of these tips include:

- Why to avoid Variant data types

- Speed up the firing of a button

- API call that is faster than Timer

- Speeding up the manipulation of Controls by using a collection

- Speeding up List Box painting

- How to test for Null string.

Avoid Redundant Code In Boolean Operations

Compatible With   **All Versions of Visual Basic**
Applies To   **Data Types**

A common error, when writing code using Boolean operations, is to perform redundant operations which simply convert a Boolean value into a Boolean value. Such operations accomplish absolutely nothing, and merely waste both code space and execution time.

Consider the following

```
Dim bVar as Boolean
If bVar = True then
    'some code...
End If
```

Since bVar is Boolean, it can have only two possible values: True or False. Likewise, the equality operator ("=") only returns two possible values: True or False. If bVar is True, the comparison returns True, and if bVar is False, the comparison returns False. So what is the point in comparing bVar to True?

Much better would be to simply say:

```
If bVar then
    ...
```

Similarly, if you want to proceed if bVar is False, you should say

```
If Not bVar Then
```

instead of

```
If bVar = False Then
```

as the Not operator is both faster and generates less code than the "=" operator.

Conversely, consider the following, where bExpression is some expression that returns a Boolean result:

```
If bExpression Then
    bVar = True
Else
    bVar = False
End If
```

Since bExpression already returns either True or False, what is the purpose of 'filtering' the result through an If?

Much better would be:

```
bVar = bExpression
```

Not only is this much smaller (and much faster), it is also a lot clearer, as it is obvious that what is intended is to set bVar equal to the result of evaluating bExpression.

For example,

```
bNotZero = x <> 0
```

not:

```
If x <> 0 Then
    bNotZero = True
Else
    bNotZero = False
End If
```

One possible cause of confusion here is that some people may not realize that the comparison operators (=, <>, <, >, <= and >=) are indeed operators that return results, just the same as the numeric operators (+, -, *, /, etc.). The only difference is that the result they return is limited to True and False (-1 and 0 in Basic). Expressions that use the relational operators can be used just the same as any other expression. There is no need to "filter" Boolean values through an If, or a comparison, to convert a Boolean value to a Boolean value!

An additional common cause of confusion is the fact that Basic uses the same symbol ("=") for both the assignment operator and the equality-comparison operator, as in:

```
bZero = x = 0
```

In this example, the first '=' is an assignment operator, which means "evaluate the expression on the right and store the result in the variable on the left." The second '=' is a comparison operator, which means "compare the subexpression on the left with the subexpression on the right and return True if they are equal and False if they are not." The compiler knows which is which because it knows whether it is scanning an expression or a statement. An expression cannot occur by itself; it must be a part of a statement. And an assignment statement has the Form 'var = expression'.

Default Variant Data Types Are Slow!

Compatible With   **All Versions of Visual Basic**
Applies To   **Data Types**

In Visual Basic Variant is the default data type. Variants are larger and 25% or more slower than other data types because Visual Basic needs to allow space for any data type you might throw at it, and it has to do a lot of work in the background.

For instance, if you use the code below:

```
Dim Data
vData = "My Data"
```

Visual Basic looks at this and says, okay, this is a string and adjusts the size of the variable appropriately. If it was done this way:

```
Dim sData as String
sData = "My Data"
```

Visual Basic knows it's a string and allocates only the space required to hold the string. More importantly, perhaps, is the fact that when Visual Basic later references the variable, it does not need to look to see what sort of data is stored in it. It's a string and that's all it could be. Variants, on the other hand, must be examined each time they're referenced to see what data type they contain.

Some programmers might use:

```
DefInt A-Z
```

to make all variables that start with the letters A through Z Integers by default. I don't recommend this. Why? Because it's a good programming practice to Dim every variable you use. There are two reasons why you should do this. One is that Visual Basic does not have to spend time deciding what type of variable it is. The other is that, during compiling, Visual Basic will check to make sure that you are putting the correct data type into a variable.

Firing A Command Button's Click Event Is Faster Than Setting Its Value Property

Compatible With   **All Versions of Visual Basic**
Applies To   **Buttons**

Some programs set a button's Value property to simulate a button click, but firing the Click event explicitly is 90% faster:

Instead of using:

```
Button1.Value = True
```

use

```
Button1_Click
```

This also makes it easy for others looking at your code to understand what's going on.

GetTickCount API Routine Is Faster Than Timer

Compatible With   **Visual Basic 3.0, Visual Basic 4.0 16-bit**
Applies To   **Timers**

The Windows API routine GetTickCount function is 85% faster than Timer. GetTickCount returns the number of milliseconds since Windows was started, and the "roll-over" point is every 49 days. The Timer's "roll-over" point is 24 hours. Since Timer only returns seconds, using GetTickCount also gives you a much higher resolution.

Declare The Following

```
Declare Function GetTickCount Lib "User"() As Long
```

Usage:

```
Dim lTimer1 as Long
lTimer1 = GetTickCount()
```

Testing For Non-Null Strings

Compatible With **All Versions of Visual Basic**
Applies To **Strings**

There are many times when you might need to test to see if a string is set to Null. This is common when dealing with database fields. Let's not confuse Null with an Empty string or a string with a zero length. Neither of these are the same as a Null string.

Some might test for Null by using

```
If sSomeString <> "" Then
```

or

```
If Len(sSomeString) = 0 Then
```

While these might work, it's 50% faster to use

```
If IsNull(sSomeString) Then
```

Check out the other "Is" operators, IsDate, IsEmpty and IsNumeric. Use the correct operator for the job you have to do.

Speeding Up Control Property Access

Compatible With **All Versions of Visual Basic**
Applies To **Controls, Forms**

Accessing a Control or Forms property many times in the same routine is very time-consuming. Because Visual Basic has to go out to the Control and get the property value each time. For example, you might do this:

```
If CheckBox1.Value = 1 'Checked Then
    'Do some code here
End If
If CheckBox1.Value = 0 'Unchecked Then
    'Do some code here
End If
```

If you just put the Value of CheckBox1 into a variable and then use it in the If statements, you greatly increase the speed.

```
Dim iValue as Integer

iValue = CheckBox1.Value
If iValue = 1 'Checked Then
    'Do some code here
ElseIf iValue = 0 'Unchecked Then
    'Do some code here
End If
```

Manipulating Controls Using The Controls Collection Is Faster Than Direct Manipulation

Compatible With   **All Versions of Visual Basic**
Applies To   **Controls**

If you have more than one control to make the same setting on, it's 10% faster to change them as a collection as opposed to individually.

Instead of doing this:

```
Command1(0).Enabled = True
Command1(1).Enabled = True
Command1(2).Enabled = True
```

do this:

```
Dim iCount as Integer
Dim I as Integer

iCount = 3
For I = 0 to iCount - 1
    Command(I).Enabled = True
Next I
```

Remember, the controls must be part of a Control Collection (the Index property must be set) for this code to work.

Turn Off List Box Painting

Compatible With   Visual Basic 3.0, Visual Basic 4.0 16-bit
Applies To   List Box

When you are loading a List Box control with information, each time you use AddItem Visual Basic adds that item to the List Box and then performs a re-paint so it can be displayed. When loading large amounts of data, this can really slow your program down. To make it ten times or more faster, turn off the re-paint. There is no property for this so we will have to use an API call.

Declare The Following

```
Declare Function SendMessage Lib "User" (ByVal hWnd _
    As Integer, ByVal wMsg As Integer, ByVal wParam _
    As Integer, lParam As Any) As Long
Const WM_SetRedraw = &HB
```

Usage

To turn off painting:

```
R = SendMessage(ListBox1.hWnd, WM_SetRedraw, 0, 0)
```

To turn painting on again:

```
R = SendMessage(ListBox1.hWnd, WM_SetRedraw, 1, 0)
```

This same method applies to any control that has an hWnd property.

Use Move Instead Of Setting Left, Top, Width And Height Properties

Compatible With   **All Version Of Visual Basic**
Applies To   **Forms, Controls**

Many of you might be setting a Form or Controls position by this method:

```
Form1.Top = 0
Form1.Left = 0
Form1.Height = 5000
Form1.Width = 7000
```

This is very slow because Visual Basic does the methods one at a time. On some machines, your users might be able to actually see this take place. Yuck! To increase the speed of this by at least 45%, use the Move method instead:

```
Form1.Move 0, 0, 5000, 7000
```

The first parameter is the Left position, the second is the Top position, the third is the Width and the fourth is the Height.

Chapter 8 — Microsoft Access

Why a chapter on Microsoft Access? Well, because most Visual Basic programmers, for better or worse, will have to deal with it. Visual Basic just happens to have a very good hook into the Access database. These tips will help you deal with this database. Some of the tips include:

- Compacting an Access database

- Checking an Access database for errors.

Checking A Database File

Compatible With   **All Versions of Visual Basic**
Applies To   **Access 2.x Database File**

Some routines that check for the existence of a file might not work with a Microsoft Access 2.0 database that is in use. To check for the file, you must open it as shared. This could be used to check a database file before it's compacted or repaired.

```
Function FileExists(Filename As String) As Integer
    On Error Resume Next
    Open Filename For Input Access Read Shared As #1
    FileExists = (Err = 0)
    Close #1
End Function
```

Also, you can use the following code to check to see if a database file is in use.

```
Function DBFileInUse(Filename As String) As Integer
    On Error Resume Next
    Open Filename For Input As #1
    DBFileInUse = (Err <> 0)
    Close #1
End Function
```

Using A Password-Protected Database

Compatible With   **Visual Basic 4 32-bit**
Applies To   **Access 7 Database**

One of the great things about Access 7 is that it's *much* easier to password-protect a database. I found a way to open a database without using INI files at all.

```
Set dbMyDatabase = OpenDatabase(Name:=App.Path & _
    "\protected-database.mdb", Exclusive:=False, _
    ReadOnly:=False, Connect:=";PWD=marvin")
```

Just provide the password as part of the connect string.

Changing The Access Title Bar

Compatible With   Microsoft Access

In Access 2.0, if you want to remove "Microsoft Access" from the Title Bar, you will need to do it the brute force way, since Microsoft provides no easy way. It's done by using the Windows API call SetWindowText.

Declare The Following

```
Declare Sub SetWindowText Lib "User" (ByVal hWnd As _
    Integer, ByVal lpString As String)
```

Code

```
Sub SetTitleText (TitleText As String)
    Dim hWnd As Integer

    'Get Access' window handle
    hWnd = GetAccessHwnd()
    If TitleText = "" Then
        'If TitleText is a zero-lengthed string, then reset
        'the Title Bar
        SetWindowText hWnd, "Microsoft Access"
    Else
        'Otherwise, set it to whatever text was
        'specified
        SetWindowText hWnd, TitleText
    End If
End Sub


Function GetAccesshWnd ()
    'Returns the handle to the Access window. FindWindow()
    'could be used, but there could be more than one
    'instance of Access, which means you could end up
    'retrieving the wrong handle. This method ensures that
    'you deal with current instance of Access.
    Dim hWnd As Integer
    Dim sBuffer As String
    Dim iCount As Integer
    Const wcAccess = "OMain"
```

```
        hWnd = GetActiveWindow()
        Do
            sBuffer = Space$(255)
            iCount = GetClassName(hWnd, sBuffer, 255)
            sBuffer = Left$(sBuffer, iCount)
            If sBuffer = wcAccess Then
                Exit Do
            End If
            hWnd = GetParent(hWnd)
            If hWnd = 0 Then
                Exit Do
            End If
        Loop
        GetAccesshWnd = hWnd
        Exit Function
    End Function
```

Compacting An Access Database

Compatible With   **Visual Basic**
Applies To   **Access 2.x Database File**

As with most databases, Access does not actually delete records when they are deleted by your program. To remove those records, you must do what Access calls "compacting". The code below can be easily added to a module and even includes code to make a backup (Access is notorious for corrupting databases at a drop of a pin). Compacting large databases can take a long time, so provide your user with a "Please wait..." type message.

NOTE: Remember, you cannot compact a database while it's open. Be sure to run this code *before* any code is run that opens the database, or any form with a data control is loaded. You could also run this at the end of your program.

```
Function bCompactMDB (sDatabase As String, _
        bBackup As Integer) As Integer
    Dim sNewFile As String
    Dim sBakFile As String

    bCompactMDB = False
    MousePointer = 11

    sNewFile = Left$(sDatabase, Len(sDatabase) - 3) & "NEW"
```

```vb
    sBakFile = Left$(sDatabase, Len(sDatabase) - 3) & "BAK"

    On Error GoTo CompactError

    If Dir(sNewFile) <> "" Then
        Kill sNewFile
    End If

    CompactDatabase sDatabase, sNewFile

    If Dir(sBakFile) <> "" Then
        Kill sBakFile
    End If

    If bBackup = True Then
        Name sDatabase As sBakFile
    End If

    If Dir(sDatabase) <> "" Then
        Kill sDatabase
    End If

    Name sNewFile As sDatabase
    bCompactMDB = True
    MousePointer = 0
    Exit Function

CompactError:
    bCompactMDB = False
    MousePointer = True
End Function
```

How To Check An Access Database For Errors

Compatible With   **Visual Basic 3.0**
Applies To   **Access Database 2.x**

One of the drawbacks to using an MS Access database in your program, is that it can corrupt very easily. Many times, there will be no warning signs or error message boxes telling you this has happened. Also, if data is entered into a database that has errors, that data (and more) might be loss forever.

Below is a Function that can be used every time a program using an Access database is loaded. This code will not catch 100% of the errors -- I have yet to discover any methods that do. In fact, I've had corrupted databases and this code did not even tell me there was an error.

This Function returns a 0 if no errors were found, or, the error code if there were.

```
Function iCheckMDB (sDatabase As String) As Integer
    Dim bDidRetry As Integer
    Dim dbTest As Database


    On Error Resume Next


    bDidRetry = False
    iCheckMDB = 0


DoOpenDatabase:
    Err = 0


    Set dbTest = OpenDatabase(sDatabase)


    If Err = 3043 Then
        'Disk or Network Error
        iCheckMDB = Err
        Exit Function
    ElseIf Err = 3049 Then
        'Database corrupted
        If Not bDidRetry Then
            'Try to repair database
            RepairDatabase sDatabase
            bDidRetry = True
            GoTo DoOpenDatabase
        Else
```

```
            iCheckMDB = Err
            Exit Function
        End If
    End If
End Function
```

NOTE: Remember to run this code before you use the database or load any forms with data controls on them.

Chapter 9 — Advanced Topics

In this chapter, we will discuss issues that are a little more involved than a tip. I call these advanced topics or subjects. These will take a little more reading and understanding. The topics I've included in this chapter are ones that you won't find anywhere else. These are subjects that every programmer will have to deal with. They are:

- What files you need to distribute with Visual Basic 4.0 program and how to install them correctly.

- How to add Windows 3.1 help files to your program

- Strategy on how to install programs into Windows 3.1

I hope that you find these articles informative.

Visual Basic 4.0 Runtime Files

Oh, I long for the days of Visual Basic 1.0, Visual Basic 2.0 and Visual Basic 3.0, when I only had to ship one runtime DLL. Well, those days are gone, starting with Visual Basic 4.0. There seems to be a lot of uncertainty about what files are required to distribute programs created with Visual Basic 4.0. Microsoft does not make this task easy for you, they just say "use the Visual Basic Setup Wizard". While most of us "seasoned" Visual Basic programmers have long stopped using the Setup Wizard (too many reasons why to list here), I've read many messages that indicate that it can't even install the required files correctly.

Below are two tables, one each for Visual Basic 4.0 16-bit and Visual Basic 4.0 32-bit. They list the minimum files required for programs to operate correctly. You will need to add to this list if you use any add-on components. As you can see from the list, there are many OLE files required.

Visual Basic 4.0 16-bit Run Time Files

File Name	Date	Size	Source	Install Settings
COMPOBJ.DLL	1/12/96	109,056	VB4\SETUPKIT\KITFILES\SYS16	Version Check Win95 Shared DLL
CTL3DV2.DLL	1/12/96	26,992	WINDOWS\SYSTEM	Version Check Win95 Shared DLL
OC25.DLL	1/12/96	536,048	WINDOWS\SYSTEM	Version Check Win95 Shared DLL Self Register
OLE2.DLL	1/12/96	304,640	VB4\SETUPKIT\KITFILES\SYS16	Version Check Win95 Shared DLL Self Register
OLE.REG	1/12/96	28,113	VB4\SETUPKIT\KITFILES\SYS16	Register
OLE2CONV.DLL	1/12/96	57,328	VB4\SETUPKIT\KITFILES\SYS16	Version Check Win95 Shared DLL
OLE2DISP.DLL	1/12/96	164,960	VB4\SETUPKIT\KITFILES\SYS16	Version Check Win95 Shared DLL
OLE2NLS.DLL	1/12/96	152,976	VB4\SETUPKIT\KITFILES\SYS16	Version Check Win95 Shared DLL
OLE2PROX.DLL	1/12/96	51,712	VB4\SETUPKIT\KITFILES\SYS16	Version Check Win95 Shared DLL
SCP.DLL	1/12/96	12,976	VB4\SETUPKIT\KITFILES\SYS16	Version Check Win95 Shared DLL
STDOLE.TLB	1/12/96	5,472	VB4\SETUPKIT\KITFILES\SYS16	
STORAGE.DLL	1/12/96	157,696	VB4\SETUPKIT\KITFILES\SYS16	Version Check Win95 Shared DLL
TYPELIB.DLL	1/12/96	177,824	VB4\SETUPKIT\KITFILES\SYS16	Version Check Win95 Shared DLL Self Register
VAEN2.DLL	1/12/96	9,136	WINDOWS\SYSTEM	Version Check Win95 Shared DLL
VAEN21.OLB	1/12/96	35,200	WINDOWS\SYSTEM	
VB40016.DLL	1/12/96	935,632	WINDOWS\SYSTEM	Version Check Win95 Shared DLL

Disk Space Required To Install Files: 2.63MB. OLE2.REG needs to be registered by using the REGEDIT program win the /s command line parameter.

Visual Basic 4.0 32-bit Run Time Files

File Name	Date	Size	Source	Install Settings
CTL3D32.DLL	3/31/96	27,136	WINDOWS\SYSTEM	Version Check Win95 Shared DLL
MSVCRT20.DLL	7/11/95	253,952	WINDOWS\SYSTEM	Version Check Win95 Shared DLL
MSVCRT40.DLL	3/31/96	326,656	WINDOWS\SYSTEM	Version Check Win95 Shared DLL
OLEPRO32.DLL	1/12/96	72,976	WINDOWS\SYSTEM	Version Check Win95 Shared DLL Self Register
VB40032.DLL	1/12/96	722,192	WINDOWS\SYSTEM	Version Check Win95 Shared DLL Self Register
VEN2232.OLB	1/12/96	37,376	WINDOWS\SYSTEM	Version Check

Disk Space Required To Install Files: 1.37MB

VB Tips & Tricks To The Rescue

If you distribute your program on-line, on the web, or just don't want to hassle with coding your install program to install the Visual Basic 4.0 runtime files, we have created 3 custom install files that will do it for you. They can be found on the VB Tips & Tricks web page and in the NicheWare forum on CompuServe.

File Name	Description
VB4RUN16.EXE	Visual Basic 4.0 16-bit run time files.
VBRUN32.EXE	Visual Basic 4.0 32-bit run time files.
VB4R32P.EXE	Visual Basic 4.0 32-bit run time files w/ MFC40.DLL (used with most OCX controls)

NOTE: All file tables are based on Visual Basic 4.0a.

What You Always Wanted To Know About Adding A Windows Help File To Your Program, But Were Afraid To Ask

So you've finished your program and your very informative and helpful Windows help file. How do you join the two together? It's not hard at all. We will discuss the easiest methods, show some cool things that can be done, along with standard things that should be included. Not much is written on this subject (in any book or manual I have access too), so this should be of interest to everyone. This article includes every function available to a programmer (that I'm aware of or could dig up).

Adding A Help File To Your Project

This is the most basic and easiest thing to do. The first thing to do is go to the [Options], [Project] menu in Visual Basic, and, in the Help File box, type in the name of the program's help file. This tells Visual Basic, which help file to use when the user presses the [F1] for help.

Now, the most time consuming thing to do is adding the HelpContextID numbers to every control that you want to access the help file. The Context ID is the reference number of a topic in the help file. Most help authoring programs (like ForeHelp and VisualHelp) will generate a report for you. If, for some reason, your authoring program does not, you can always look at the file with the .HH extension. They are listed there.

There are two ways to actually add the Context ID numbers. The first is to type them right into the HelpContextID property of most controls. While this is the easiest, if the Context ID number changes in the help file, your controls will no longer bring up the correct topic.

The second way is to add them by code. While this will take more time, it's safer and will save you time in the long run. Most help authoring programs will produce a text or BAS file that looks like this:

```
Global Const CONTENTS = 1025
Global Const VBWIN = 1168
Global Const Buttons_Image = 1016
Global Const Detecting_End_of_Drag_Drops_Sequences = 1036
Global Const Image_Control_As_Button = 1078
Global Const Mouse_Button_Up_Or_Down = 1101
Global Const _
     Placing_The_Cursor_On_The_Button_That_Has_Focus = 1115
```

Somewhere in your code, before you show the Form, add the following code:

```
Command1.HelpContextID = Mouse_Button_Up_Or_Down
Command2.HelpContextID = Buttons_Image
```

Using either of these methods, when the user presses [F1], whatever control has the focus determines what topic will be displayed.

Cleaning Up When Your Program Unloads

Unfortunately, when your program closes, Visual Basic does not automatically close the associated help file(s). It's a good idea to do this, but you will need to use a WinHelp API call. First, you declare the following lines in a module:

```
Declare Function WinHelp Lib "User" (ByVal hWnd As _
     Integer, ByVal lpHelpFile As String, ByVal wCommand _
     As Integer, ByVal dwData As Any) As Integer
Global Const HELP_QUIT = &H2
```

Then, use the following call in your program exit procedure:

```
Dim R as Integer
R = WinHelp(Form1.hWnd, "MYHELP.HLP", HELP_QUIT, CLng(0))
```

If the help file is not running, no error will occur.

Now For Some Standard Things To Include In The Program

It's good to follow some guidelines and include some standard items in your help menu. You should provide a way for users to access the Contents of your help file (usually the main page) and a way for users to access the Search box in the help file to look up items quickly. Also, for those users who are not familiar with how a help file works, include a way for them to get to the "How To Use Help" file that comes with Windows.

Here's how to do it. Use the same declare statement in the section above. Also add the following constants:

```
Global Const HELP_CONTENTS = &H3
Global Const HELP_PARTIALKEY = &H105
Global Const HELP_HELPONHELP = &H4
```

Now for the code. To go to the Contents topic of your help file, use:

```
R = WinHelp(Form1.hWnd, "MYHELP.HLP", _
    HELP_CONTENTS, CLng(0))
```

The Contents topic of your help file can be changed on the fly.

To bring up the search dialog box, use:

```
R = WinHelp(Form1.hWnd, "MYHELP.HLP", HELP_PARTIALKEY, "")
```

You can also pre-search for a word by replacing the empty string with word string. If the entire search word is found, and there is only one topic that uses that keyword, then the topic will be displayed instead of the search dialog box.

To bring up "How To Use Help", use:

```
R = WinHelp(Form1.hWnd, "", HELP_HELPONHELP, CLng(0))
```

Now For The Cool Things You Can Do

While most programs should include the items mentioned above, there is a list of functions that are available to your program. Some are really cool! We will cover everything (that I'm aware of) that can be done and how to program them.

Invoking The Help File Using A Context ID:

This is just like pressing [F1] on a control that has the HelpContextID property set to a Context ID number. There might be instances in your program that you might want to manually do this.

```
Global Const HELP_CONTEXT = &H1
R = WinHelp(Form1.hWnd, "MYHELP.HLP", HELP_CONTEXT, _
    CLng(1001))
```

The last parameter is the Context ID number.

Changing The Help File Contents Topic:

The Contents of your help file is normally the topic that was set to be the contents topic when the help file was compiled. But your program can change the Contents to be a different topic during runtime. This can be useful if you have one help file for multiple programs. Simply use the code below and, in the last parameter, fill in the new context ID number.

```
Global Const HELP_SETCONTENTS = &H5
R = WinHelp(Form1.hWnd, "MYHELP.HLP", _
    HELP_SETCONTENTS, ByVal CLng(1001))
```

Changing the Contents index can only be done while the help file is loaded. Also, once the help file is closed, then the Contents index reverts back to normal.

Popup Help For Your Program:

Adding quick help to your programs is getting easier these days with the ever popular "Balloon Help" that is seen in almost all major programs. This same type of quick help is easily added to Visual Basic programs with the help of a few popular VBXes. The problem is that most of this help is just a word or two. What if you want to give the user a little more help and use graphics, without making them go all the way into the program's help file? It's much easier than you would think. You can add the same pop-up help capability to your program that is available in help files. And it's trivial!

Declare the following:

```
Global Const HELP_CONTEXTPOPUP = &H8
```

Follow this sample code:

```
Sub Command1_MouseDown (Button As Integer, Shift As _
        Integer, X As Single, Y As Single)
    Dim R As Integer

    'Right Mouse Click
    If Button = 2 Then
        R = WinHelp(Form1.hWnd, "MYHELP.HLP", _
            HELP_CONTEXTPOPUP, Clng(1005))
    End If
End Sub
```

The pop-up help will stay on the screen until the user presses any mouse button or key (just like a help file). The last parameter is the Context ID number.

Search For A Keyword:

Using this function will invoke the help file and bring up a topic based on a predefined keyword for that topic. The keywords are the same ones that appear in the Search dialog box.

```
Global Const HELP_KEY = &H101
R = WinHelp(Form1.hWnd, "MYHELP.HLP", HELP_KEY, "Index")
```

One warning when using this function. If the keyword is not found, then an error will occur. It might be better to use the HELP_PARTIALKEY function. If the keyword is found with HELP_PARTIALKEY, the associated topic will be displayed, otherwise the search dialog box will be invoked.

Setting The Position Of The Help File

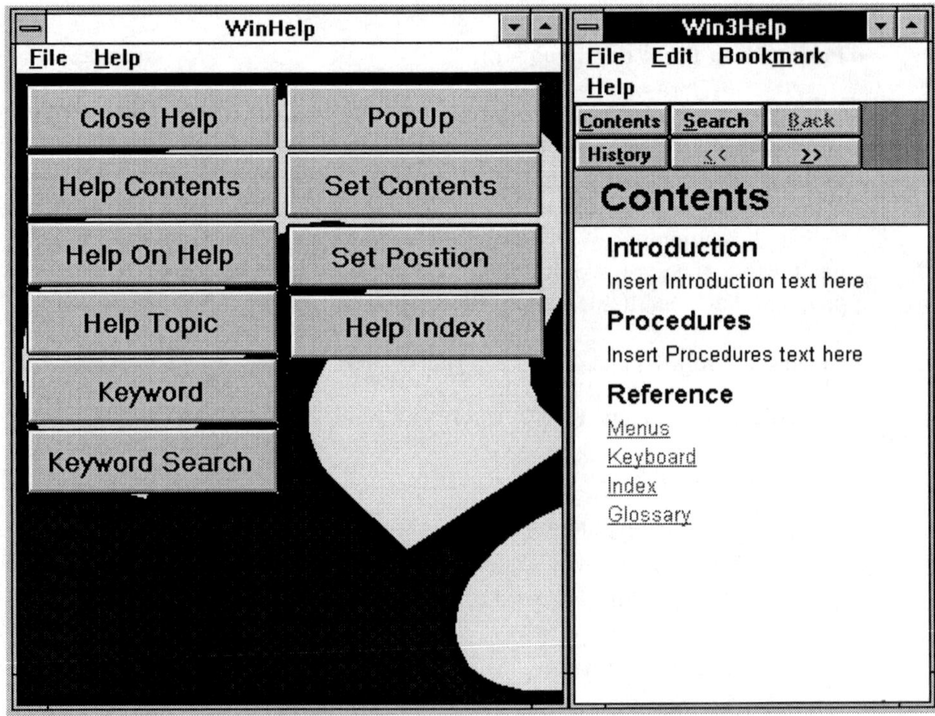

Instead of displaying the help file at the default position, you might want to position it so it does not cover up your program, as shown in the graphic. This is a little tricky to do. We will need to create a new WinHelp call so that we can pass it a Type. The Type that we will pass will be filled with the top, left, width and height coordinates, length of the structure, and the window name.

First, declare the following:

```
Type HELPWININFO '12 bytes + length of rgchMember
    wStructSize As Integer
    x As Integer
    y As Integer
    dx As Integer
    dy As Integer
    wMax As Integer
    rgchMember As String * 2 'Length varies depending on the
    window name
End Type


Global Const HELP_SETWINPOS = &H203
Global Const SW_HIDE = 0
Global Const SW_SHOWNORMAL = 1
Global Const SW_SHOWMINIMIZED = 2
Global Const SW_SHOWMAXIMIZED = 3
Global Const SW_SHOWNOACTIVATE = 4
Global Const SW_SHOW = 5
Global Const SW_MINIMIZE = 6
Global Const SW_SHOWMINNOACTIVE = 7
Global Const SW_SHOWNA = 8
Global Const SW_RESTORE = 9


Declare Function WinHelpType Lib "User" Alias _
    "WinHelp" (ByVal hWnd As Integer, ByVal lpHelpFile _
    As String, ByVal wCommand As Integer, dwData As Any) _
    As Integer
```

The HELPWININFO type is fourteen bytes, as defined above. The x and y parameters are the upper left corner of the new position. The dx and dy parameters are the width and height of the help file window. The SW_ constants are used in the wMax parameter to determine how the help file will be displayed. Normally, you would use the SW_SHOWNORMAL constant. The rgchMember parameter is the window name. I'm not sure what this is used for, but passing it an empty string works just fine.

There is something very important about the positioning and size of the help file when using this function. The coordinates are NOT in pixels or even twips (good one, guys). The WinHelp engine uses a coordinate system of 1024x1024, regardless of the screen resolution. You will need to convert pixels or twips to coincide with this. The sample code that comes on the disks that came with this book has already done this for you!

Now, here is some sample code to use the positioning functions:

```
Dim NewPos As HELPWININFO

NewPos.wStructSize = 12
NewPos.x = 10
NewPos.y = 10
NewPos.dx = 100
NewPos.dy = 100
NewPos.wMax = SW_SHOWNORMAL
NewPos.rgchMember = ""


R = WinHelpType(Form1.hWnd, "MYHELP.HLP", _
    HELP_SETWINPOS, NewPos)
```

This function does create a really cool effect.

Forcing A File To Display

This setting will simply force the specified help file to display, if it is not already being displayed. This is useful if you want to make sure the help file gets displayed, but you don't want it to go to the Contents topic, if the user is on another topic. If the help file is not already loaded, then it will be displayed on the Contents topic.

```
Global Const HELP_COMMAND = &H102
R = WinHelp(Form1.hWnd, "MYHELP.HLP", _
    HELP_FORCEFILE, CLng(0))
```

Invoking A Macro

Another cool feature is that you can invoke a Windows Help macro. For example, you can copy a topic to the clipboard or even print a topic. Remember though, the help file needs to be loaded before you send the macro. Note the different WinHelp function call.

```
HELP_COMMAND = &H102
sMacro="CopyDialog()"
R = WinHelpString(Form1.hWnd, "MYHELP.HLP", _
    HELP_COMMAND, sMacro)
```

Multikey Tables

Last but not least is the ability to use a different keyword table in a help file. The only reason this is last is that I do not have a help file that uses this feature, so I can't test it. But, the ability is there. Using this function will assign a different keyword table as default. Note the different WinHelp function.

```
Dim MultiKey As MULTIKEYHELP

MultiKey.mkSize = 256
MultiKey.mkKeyList = "A"
MultiKey.szKeyphrase = "Add"

R = WinHelpType(Form1.hWnd, "MYHELP.HLP", _
    HELP_MULTIKEY, MultiKey)
```

Wrap Up

There are two constants I did not discuss. They are HELP_INDEX and HELP_SETINDEX. These are the same as HELP_CONTENTS and HELP_SETCONTENTS. They are left over from the Windows 3.0 help engine.

Well, there you have it! Everything you can do with a help file from your program! I've created a sample program that uses all of the above function calls and a module to wrap up this code for easy use by any program. You can find it by downloading it from CompuServe. Type NICHEWARE and download WIN3HELP.ZIP in library #9.

I must give credit where credit is due. Some of the information above came from Daniel Appleman's book "Visual Basic Programmer's Guide To The Windows API". While the book did not tell me everything I wanted to know, it did get me started.

Program Install and Setup Strategy for Windows 3.1

A user's first experience with your software begins when he runs the installation program. If your installation is inadequate and/or bug-ridden, the user will not be impressed and will likely carry that negative impression over to your application itself.

Over the years, I've developed a set of steps to follow in order produce an installation program that works well. Those six steps are given below.

Also, you should seriously consider writing a setup program for your products early in their development cycle. If you wait until the end and rush this very important step, you will be in for major headaches. I always include an install program with beta versions of my software. This way, beta testers test not only test the program but the install as well.

Step 1: Find A Well-Written and Easy To Use Installation Utility

This is paramount to the success of your installation. Do not write one yourself! The hundred dollars or so you save will not be worth the time you will need to put into it. Also, delete the Setup Wizard that comes with Visual Basic 3.0! It's slow, buggy and just a waste of disk space. Don't bother with it at all. There are many very good setup programs out there. Just ask around and you will find one that suits your needs.

Step 2: Make A List Of Files Needed For The Installation

Believe it or not, this is one of the hardest things to do in Visual Basic. With add-on products that use DLLs, VBXes, and database engines, it's very difficult to find out what your program really is using. Here is a step-by-step method that I use:

Start with the Visual Basic Project Window. There you will find a list of VBXes that your program uses. First make sure your program is actually using them. Visual Basic adds many default VBXes, that you might never use. To make sure, simply click on the VBX name in the Project Window, then click on File followed by Remove File. If the VBX is currently in use, you will get an error message. Once you have made this list, refer to the manual for the VBX for any additional DLLs, license files, or other files that need to be shipped with it. This might take some digging. Most VBX vendors, for some reason, don't provide a list, or, make it difficult to find. If the manual doesn't tell you what files are required for a control, call the vendor.

Check Modules For DLLs. Besides the DLLs that VBXes might use, your program might reference some with Declare Sub and Declare Function API calls. Of course, you don't need to include files like Kernel, because it comes with Windows.

Include Database Drivers. These files won't be listed anywhere in your project. Be sure to consult your database manual for a list of files needed. For a list of some of these files, see the "Required DLLs for Distributing Visual Basic Applications" topic in the Visual Basic 3.0 help file. You can also refer to the SETUPWIZ.INI (the only piece of the Setup Wizard that worth keeping) for a list of additional files needed.

Don't Forget SHARE.EXE. If your program uses a database, then you will also need to install SHARE.EXE (found in the Windows or DOS directory). This is not needed for Windows for Workgroups. Also, consult your database manual for SHARE parameters needed for that database. For instance, when using MS Access, you need to add "SHARE.EXE /L:500" to the user's AUTOEXEC.BAT file.

Include VBRUN300.DLL, Too. Of course, you will need to include the Visual Basic run-time file. Make sure you have the latest version. New versions can be downloaded from CompuServe, the MS BBS, Microsoft's Web site, or numerous FTP sites around the world

Add Any Additional Files Your Program Needs. Last but not least, add any other files your program requires to run. These can include database files, help files, graphic files, INI files etc. This also includes OLE files if needed.

Don't Forget The DLL For IIF. If you use the IIF statement in Visual Basic, then you will need to include the financial functions DLL, MSAFINX.DLL. This is a very common file to forget, probably because MS does not mention it in the Visual Basic help file at all!

Step 3: Double-Check Your File List

Now that you have your list of files, you need to double-check it. The only good way to do this is to use a program that comes with Visual Basic that you probably don't know about. It's called the Windows Process Status program. The executable is called WPS.EXE. You'll find it tucked away in the CDK directory. This program has saved me countless hours in tracking down programs and files that are in use.

WPS will list all EXE files, DLLs, VBXes that are currently in use on your system. It will even tell you their versions and the directory they were loaded from. Put this program in a group in Program Manager -- you will use it often.

Okay, how can WPS help you? Here is what I do: Make sure Visual Basic and your program are not loaded. Rebooting Windows will help clean out any unwanted side effects. Start WPS and do a Save Dump to a file. Start your program and make sure you go through all the forms so that VBXes and DLLs will load. Click Update! on WPS and save the result with another Save Dump.

Open up both files side by side in Notepad and compare the lists. This list should match your VBX, EXE, DLL list you made previously. If it doesn't, then you need to do some more digging and testing. Using WPS is almost 100% accurate.

Step 4: Decide Where Files Should Be Installed

I'm going to get a lot of mail on this section, but hear me out. There is a method to my madness. Contrary to what Microsoft or other magazines might tell you, 99% of the time commonly used files should not be placed in the WINDOWS\SYSTEM directory. Why? Simply because of version control. Unfortunately, many install programs (and/or programmers) do not practice good version control. What does this mean to you? If someone installs a VBX or DLL that is a different, incompatible version with your program... *your* program will not work and *you* will get a technical support call.

Generally, 99.99% of DLLs and VBXes do not need to be installed into the WINDOWS\SYSTEM directory. The MS dream of programs sharing and using components in Windows 3.1 is still a dream. It does not work. I wanted to believe in it, it makes sense, but it is just not practical at this time. So what do you do? Simple, install all DLLs, VBXes, and related files into your program directory. This way you have control over exactly what your program uses. I even install VBRUN300.DLL because there have been a couple of upgrades to it. There, the version control problem is solved. Or is it?

There is one vast wasteland you will have to take into account. Memory! Installing all files into the program directory is 100% foolproof, except if another program is currently using a different version VBX or DLL before your program is loaded. Because, Windows checks to see if a file is in memory before it loads it from disk. If it's there, it does not load it again. This is the only place your program could run into problems.

Don't fret, there is a solution... check memory for incompatible file version before your program loads any forms or modules. If the incompatible file is in memory then you can warn the user. Checking memory for files is pretty easy using simple API calls that are built right into Windows. Okay, you might not agree with me on this theory, but I have NEVER gotten a technical support calls because of file version problems using this method.

Step 5: Now It's Time To Put Together The Installation

Here is where your installation utility comes in. I won't go into specifics here because every program is different. I also don't want to sound like an advertisement for a particular program, so I'm just going to go over some major points:

Make Your Installation Fun. Installations don't have to be boring or a pain. Make it fun by adding graphics, sounds and even text explaining features of the program. Remember, this is the first thing your customer sees, so make a good impression!

Give The User The Power Of Choice. People like to feel they are in control, so don't install the program into a pre-configured directory or Program Manager group. Let them choose. Of course, you really should provide appropriate defaults. For larger programs, if appropriate, let them install with custom options.

Don't Bug The User Too Much. Don't make too many choices or go through too many screens before the program installs. They will be exhausted before your program is even used. What I mean by this is, **you** do the work of finding things such as the WINDOWS\SYSTEM directory, if SHARE.EXE is loaded, or if they have enough disk space, memory, files/buffers settings, etc. You can even search for a previous version of your program to pre-determine the default location where your program should be installed. Just remember to not ask the user for any information you can find yourself.

Install As Quickly As Possible. People don't want to wait for an hour to install a program. So make sure you use a program to create an installation program that is FAST! This is one major reason not to use Setup Wizard. This is a true story... I installed a program that used the Setup Wizard that spanned three disks. It took almost an hour on a P90!

Version Check, Version Check, Version Check, Version Check. I can't stress this enough! Use an installation utility that incorporates version checking. This is not an option. Set the program to version check every file that includes version information. If you are unsure about a file, just click on it from File Manger, and then click on Files, then Properties. This will list all version information, if it's available. Also, set the program to overwrite the file if it's the same version or older. This way, if a file gets corrupted, your install will overwrite it with a good copy. This is also needed if your VBX vendor forgot to update the version number in their software. This has happened, and you know who you are.

Use An Uninstall Option. One of the biggest fears that users have about install programs is what it's going to do to their system. We all know that installing one program could wreak havoc to your system that could take hours or even days to correct. So, at least create an install log of what your program did to the system. This includes INI, AUTOEXEC.BAT and CONFIG.SYS file changes. At best, provide an uninstall program that will read the log file and do what it takes to leave the user's computer the way you found it. At the beginning of my install, I always let the user know that I've included an uninstall program. I even put it in the Program Manager Group along with the program icon

Create A Good Ending. There are a few things that you need or can do at the end of the installation:

Thank The User. I always thank the user for installing the program. I know that installs are scary for some people, so I always want to be friendly.

Display Read Me Or Help Files. It's a good idea to give the user some insight on the new version features, how to purchase products etc. This can be done by either displaying a readme file or a topic page from the application help file.

Offer To Reboot. If you installed files, or changed settings in the autoexex.bat or CONFIG.SYS or other files that require Windows or the PC to be rebooted, offer to do it for the user. Make sure you do not force this issue. They might have some programs open that need to closed first.

Start The Program. Offer to start the newly installed program for them. This way they can start using it right away.

Use SETUP.EXE. When you create the file that starts the installation process, use the name SETUP.EXE. Do not use INSTALL.EXE or any other name. SETUP.EXE is the standard name used by all Windows programs. People have come to know this and look for it on disks. Using any other name may confuse your users.

Also don't forget to print Instructions on the disk label. Make sure you print easy to understand instructions on the label of the #1 disk. Don't rely on the user to know what to do. If your program can be installed on different OSes, print instructions for each one.

Step 6: Test, Test and Test The Install!

Before you start shipping, test the install program as much as you can! This step is VERY important. The last thing you need is to duplicate hundreds or thousands of disks and then find out it does not always work. Here are some steps to remember:

Test Different Operating Systems. One hopes that during the writing of your install program, you made it compatible with every different OS that you support. You also need to take into consideration Windows 95. The install procedures and practices are very different.

Use A Clean Machine. Make sure that you test the install on a "virgin" machine for each OS. This simply means that your install program has never been run on it. The ideal situation is to have a machine that has typical installation of the OS. This makes sure that you have not forgotten any files when you later test your program. Not everyone has the luxury of many different computers sitting around. You may have only your development machine. In this case, make sure you delete or move all files that your installation program will install into a directory that is not in the Path statement. Also, make sure to delete any INI, AUTOEXEC.BAT and CONFIG.SYS file settings you might make. If at all possible, do not test your install or your program on your development machine. Everything always seems to work on that machine and, most of the time, not on others.

Have Others Test It. This is another important step. Get the install into as many different hands as time allows. No matter how much you have tested it, others might have problems. It's better to work it out before it ships!

Test Your Program. Last but not least, make sure you test your program after it's installed. This will double-check that all required files were installed correctly and all appropriate settings work! If you include an uninstall program, test that too. Make sure it totally cleans up after itself.

Conclusion

Well, there you have it. In a nutshell, those are the steps I use for every program. Generally, if I follow these guidelines, I never have a problem. Of course, your install needs might be different, but the six steps listed above should make it easier for you.

Chapter 10 — Third-Party Components

This chapter contains tips and tricks for third-party Visual Basic add-on components. This chapter is not here to promote any of these products, just to give you unpublished tips on a component. In this chapter, we have tips on:

- THREED.VBX from Sheridan

- CSCALNDR.VBX from Crescent Software

- VSVBX from VideoSoft

- TrueGrid from TrueGrid

Enable/Disable A 3D Command Button Using A Single Graphic

Here's a handy way to enable/disable a 3D command button without creating separate images. The function is based on converting gray to black and vice versa, so make sure that your original pictures (the enabled images) do not contain gray parts, or they will be converted to black when re-enabled.

This function uses a picture box. Just place some picture box on any Form and set the visible property to false.

Declare The Following

```
Declare Function GetPixel Lib "GDI" (ByVal hDC As Integer, _
    ByVal X As Integer, ByVal Y As Integer) As Long
Declare Function SetPixel Lib "GDI" (ByVal hDC As Integer, _
    ByVal X As Integer, ByVal Y As Integer, ByVal crColor _
    As Long) As Long
```

Code

```
Sub Enable3DButton (Cmd3D As Control, SrcPicture As _
    Control, Enable As Integer)
Dim Color As Long
Dim RetVal As Long
Dim X As Integer
Dim Y As Integer
    SrcPicture.AutoSize = True
    SrcPicture.ScaleMode = 3    'Pixels
    SrcPicture.AutoRedraw = True
    Cmd3D.Enabled = Enable
    If Not Enable Then
        SearchColor = 0
        ReplaceColor = 8
    Else
        SearchColor = 8
        ReplaceColor = 0
    End If
    SrcPicture.Picture = Cmd3D.Picture
    For Y = 0 To SrcPicture.ScaleHeight - 1
        For X = 0 To SrcPicture.ScaleWidth - 1
```

```
            Color = GetPixel(SrcPicture.hDC, X, Y)
            If Color = QBColor(SearchColor) Then
                RetVal = SetPixel(SrcPicture.hDC, X, _
                    Y, QBColor(ReplaceColor))
            End If
        Next
    Next
    Cmd3D.Picture = SrcPicture.Image
End Sub
```

Setting The Date In CSCALNDR.VBX

If you try setting the date of the CSCALNDR VBX that comes in QuickPak Pro using the following code:

```
CSCALNDR1 = Now
```

The calendar will roll over to the next day at noon! It's 12 hours off. The Now function returns a double precision number, but CSCALNDR is expecting an integer and incorrectly converts the double. By using the Fix function which returns an integer, you can easily solve this problem.

```
CSCALNDR1 = Fix(Now)
```

Use Fewer Label Controls With The VSVBX Elastic Control

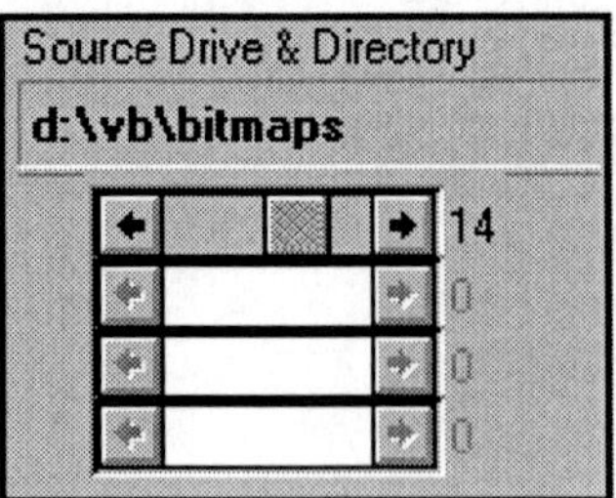

We all know that one of the things that really slows down the loading of a Visual Basic form is the number of controls on it. If you can decrease this number, then it will load and paint faster! Most data-entry type controls (Text Boxes) need to have a label control next to them telling the user what the Text Box is for. If you have 25 Text Boxes, boom, you have just doubled the number of controls by adding 25 labels too. What's the solution?

It's easy. The VSVBX control from VideoSoft has a control called an Elastic control. I won't go into all the cool things this control can do, but it does give you the ability to "fake" label boxes (as seen in the graphic above). The text above the drive info is not a label. The number next to the scroll bar is not a label.

You place the text you want displayed next to a control in the Tag property of that control. By using the CaptionPosition, CaptionStyle, TagPosition and TagWidth properties in the Elastic control, you can position the label at any position above, to the right and to the left of the referenced control. You can even make it 3D!

Remember, when you change the Tag property (like in the scroll bars in the graphic above), you need to force the Elastic to re-paint by sending it a Refresh so it will display the new text..

Since all my projects use VSVBX anyway, this is a really "cool" feature that makes my programs load faster.

How To Fill The TrueGrid Built-in Combo Box With Data

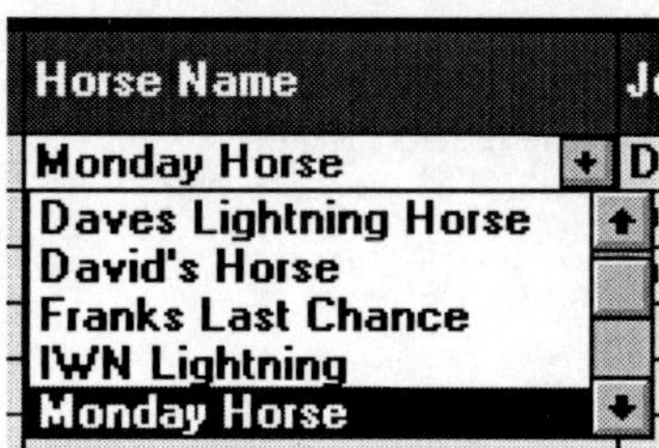

If you want to add a drop-down Combo Box to TrueGrid, the help file suggests using another grid for the data and make it visible when the user clicks on the cell. While this is fine if you need to display more than one column of data, it's a waste of resources for simple lists. Why not use the drop-down Combo Box that is built right into TrueGrid?

Even though the drop-down box needs a few minor improvements (like automatically dropping down when the user starts to edit the column), it is very functional. You can even show a name (see graphic) but really be using an ID number. The name is just referenced by the Combo Box to the ID number.

In the sample code below (straight from one of my projects), you will see how to add both the name and the ID number. I set the Combo Box using the VlistStyle property. The GVLS_TRANSLATE setting sets it to translate the ID number to a name, the GVLS_SORTCOMBO sorts the Combo Box and finally the GVLS_COMBO sets it as a Combo Box.

```
Sub FillHorseList ()
    Dim I As Integer
    Dim dbList As database
    Dim ssList As snapshot
    Dim sSql As String

    tblMain.VlistColumn = 3
    tblMain.VlistStyle = GVLS_TRANSLATE + GVLS_SORTCOMBO + _
        GVLS_COMBO
    I = 1

    sSql = "SELECT DISTINCTROW tblHorse.HorseID, " & _
        "tblHorse.Name FROM tblHorse ORDER BY " & _
        "tblHorse.Name;"
    Set dbList = OpenDatabase(gDataDir & "VPDATA.MDB", _
        False, True)
```

```
        Set ssList = dbList.CreateSnapshot(sSql)

    ssList.MoveFirst

    Do Until ssList.EOF
        tblMain.VlistData(I) = ssList!HorseID
        tblMain.VlistText(I) = ssList!Name
        I = I + 1
        ssList.MoveNext
    Loop

    ssList.Close
    dbList.Close
End Sub
```

Appendix A

VB Tips & Tricks Newsletter

The tips contained in this newsletter are derived from the VB Tips & Tricks newsletter. This electronic publication was started in September of 1993 and is published bi-monthly. The disks that come with this book have a recent version of the newsletter.

Each month the newsletter adds more:

- Tips and tricks

- Advanced articles

- Component reviews

- Component product information

- Component and Visual Basic bugs

- Visual Basic and Component News

- Sample code

- Custom programs, modules and classes

- And much much more. VB Tips & Tricks is downloaded by 50,000+ programmers every month, so we must be doing something right!

VB Tips & Tricks is a powerful publication because it's written by many, many programmers just like you that freely share their knowledge with others. VB Tips & Tricks is the vehicle to help them do just that.

Even though you can download the latest issue of VB Tips & Tricks free from the web site (http://www.apexsc.com/Visual Basic/nw/Visual Basictt.html), it does not contain:

- Tips & Tricks except from the current year.

- Custom programs, modules and classes

To stay updated with these two very important features, you will need to purchase a subscription. If you do, each issue can be mailed to you, e-mailed to you or you can download a patch program from the web site. Also, by subscribing you are helping to keep the newsletter going.

To subscribe contact:

Mabry Software, Inc.
PO Box 31926
Seattle, WA 98103-1926

Phone: 206-634-1443
Fax: 206-632-0272
E-Mail: mabry@mabry.com
Web: www.mabry.com

Price List:

E-Mail $60 ($65 outside of North America)
Postal Delivery $100 ($120 outside of North America)
(Prices subject to change without notice.)

Appendix B

VB Tips & Tricks Web Site

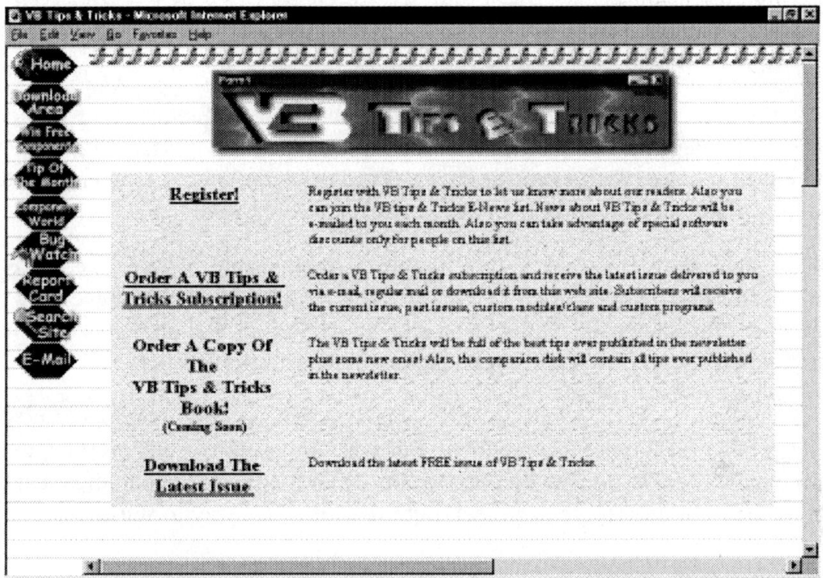

To continue to help programmers, we have set up a website for the newsletter. The URL is **http://www.apexsc.com/vb/nw/vbtt.html**. This web site is dedicated to further helping programmers. Here are the major sections:

Download Area

The download area is there to allow readers to download the latest and greatest issues of the newsletter. Subscribers can even download a small patch to their current issue.

There are also other files, like the VB Tips & Tricks screen saver, required runtime files for Visual Basic 4.0, and more.

VB Tips & Tricks Report Cards

Probably the most useful area on the site is the VB Tips & Tricks Report Cards. This area helps programmers choose the best component products around.

VB Tips & Tricks Report Card Vision

Since there are now so many vendors creating components for Visual Basic, it's hard for a developer to know what to buy. There are many factors in purchasing components that we hope to take care of in this area.

If you are like me, your boss walks into your office and tells you that the program you are currently working on needs a new feature added right away (he really means yesterday)! You scramble to check your stack of magazines and marketing material. More often than not, you don't have time to devote days or weeks into researching a component. You have to make your best choice within a few hours.

Marketing material can tell you about features but not the quality of the component. Reviews in magazines are better, but most of the time those reviews are written by people who have used the component for only a few days -- not nearly long enough to really tell you how the component works in a real project.

This is where the VB Tips & Tricks Report Card comes in! Programmers like you submit a grade (and can change their grade at any time). And like you, they have used the component for longer than a few days and are using it in real projects. They have a first hand knowledge of how the component "really" performs.

So, not only does the VB Tips & Tricks Report Card give you the opportunity to let your feelings be known about a component, but you can use it as "the" resource to choose a good component. There is no way that this or any other method can guarantee that a component will be the right one for your project, but this is the best way to start!

Grading A Component

When you go to this HTML form you can grade any one of 500+ products from our database. After selecting a product, you then grade it on:

- Give it a Final Grade

- Suitability To Task

- Technically Sound

- Ease Of Use

- Documentation

- Bang For The Buck

- Technical Support

- Install/Uninstall & Setup

You also have the opportunity to make comments and suggestions on the product. The grade gets sent to VB Tips & Tricks and, about once a week, the new results are posted.

Report Card Results

#6 - Wise Installation System	
Report Card	Vendor: Great Lakes Business Solutions Inc.
Final Grade — A	Price: $199 + S&H
Install/Uninstall & Setup — A +	Phone: 3139814970
Ease Of Use — A	E-mail: 75111.606@compuserve.com
Suitability To Task — A	WWW URL: www.glbs.com
Technically Sound — A -	Component Category: Installation Programs
Documentation — B -	
Technical Support — A -	Description:
Bang For The Buck — A	The Wise Installation System is a Windows-based installation editor that quickly creates installation programs for Windows, Windows 95, and Windows NT. The installations are created as a single EXE file (one file per disk for multiple-disk installations). Wise supports calls to DLL-based functions, checking for DLL/VBX dependencies, and bitmap graphics. A demo version is available on Great Lakes' BBS, on CompuServe (GO WISEINSTALL), and on GLBS's World Wide Web site.
GRADES SUBMITTED= 34	

About once a week, all the new grades are entered into a database. Then the components are given an overall grade based on the average in each category. You can then view the following:

Top Ten Page. The top ten products are listed here.

Bottom Ten Page. The products with the worst scores are listed on this page.

All Components. Here you can choose by category the products for which you want to see the grade.

So come to the Report Card area to grade components and also make a more informed decision on what product to purchase.

VB Tips & Tricks Bug Watch™

This section is dedicated to providing timely information about major problems that exist in component software. Programmers submit most of the bugs after exhausting all other avenues. So check this page our before purchasing any component software!

Component World

This section contains a lot of useful information about component software for Visual Basic. The major sections of this area are:

Review of the Month: Read a review of the hottest component software around. These reviews are usually published before the review is released in the newsletter.

Bug Watch™: Same as described above.

Report Cards: Same as described above.

Component Information: Information on the components made by the vendors that advertise with VB Tips & Tricks.

Component Vendor Web Sites: The URL's for the vendors that advertise with VB Tips & Tricks.

Win Free Components: Every month we give away component software to one or more lucky person that submits a tip to the newsletter.

Other Areas

There is much more to see at the site, like "Tip of the Month", site search and more. You will just have to explore it and have fun.

Appendix C   Other Sources Of Help

You are very lucky. Back when I started programming in Visual Basic, there was very little help available. The Visual Basic books weren't much help and there was no where else to turn. Things have changed! There is a lot of information available now. In this section, I will list all sorts of resources that I would highly recommend and are currently using or have used in the past. You can not go wrong with any of these sources.

Books

There are actually very few books out there that are worth the 40 plus dollars most publishing houses want for them. Here is a list of books that should be on just about everyone's bookshelf.

The Visual Basic Programmer's Guide To the Win32

By: Daniel Appleman
Published By: Ziff-Davis Press
ISBN: 1-56276-287-7. 1518 pages. $49.99 US

This is a must-have for any programming using Windows 95 or Windows NT. If you are going to use 32-bit API calls, then you need this book!

Visual Basic Programmer's Guide to the Windows API

By: Daniel Appleman
Published By: Ziff-Davis Press
ISBN: 1-56276-073-4. $34.95 US

If you are programming in Windows 3.1 and using API calls, then you need this book too!

Doing Objects In Microsoft Visual Basic 4.0

By: Deborah Kurata
Published By: Ziff-Davis Press
ISBN: 1-56276-337-7 $39.95 US

If you are new to Visual Basic or new to object-oriented programming then this is the book for you. Deborah explains the methodology behind object-oriented programming, how to apply it, and how to use it in Visual Basic 4.

Visual Basic 4.0 Internet Programming

By: Carl Franklin
Published By: John Wiley & Sons, Inc.
ISBN: 0-471-13420-1 $39.95 US

Most of you will be getting into some type of Internet programming. In this book, Carl explains WinSock programming, E-mail programming, and more.

Visual Basic Programmer's Guide To Serial Communications

By: Dick Grier
Published By: Mabry Publishing
ISBN: 1-890422-25-8 $34.95 US

Add serial communcations to your Visual Basic applications using custom controls and the Windows API. Here is the information that you need to use modems and direct serial connections (including RS-232, RS-422 and RS-485) for almost any purpose.

Richard Grier uses his many years of experience to guide you through the process, while providing the insight that you will need to extend and adapt the ideas that he presents to your own projects.

About Face: The Essentials of User Interface Design

By: Alan Cooper
Publised By: IDG Books Worldwide
ISBN: 1-56884-322-4 $29.99

Alan Cooper is considered the "father of Visual Basic". From what I've heard, he actually wrote the first Visual Basic prototype and sold it to our friend Bill Gates. Anyway, Alan is now into user interface and this book is a must have! Alan will help you write a better interface, which is a *very* important piece of your programs. Alan is also just about the best speaker I have ever had the pleasure of hearing. If you can, catch him at the next Visual Basic Insiders Technical Summit. Just listening to him is well worth the ticket.

Publications

Visual Basic Programmers Journal

This magazine has always been the best one out there for Visual Basic programmers. It's published each month with some extra issues thrown in. It also comes on CD. You can subscribe by calling 800-848-5523 or visit their web site at http://www.windx.com.

Web Sites

There are so many web sites dealing with Visual Basic, it's tough to find the good ones. Here are my favorites.

Carl & Gary's Visual Basic Home Page

These guys have always had the largest selection of Visual Basic related links and component vendor information. It also has information on User Groups, List Servers, Use Groups and much more. It's the first site I go to when I'm looking for information. The URL is http://www.apexsc.com/Visual Basic.

Microsoft's Visual Basic Page

While this page does not offer a lot of content, it is maintained by Microsoft and has the latest breaking news about Visual Basic and all the current program updates and download. The URL is http://www.microsoft.com/Visual Basicasic.

User Groups

Another fantastic place to get help is your local Visual Basic user group. I help run the one here in San Diego. We average about 70 programmers each month ranging from experienced to those who have not even bought Visual Basic yet. Find the one near you and get involved, you will not regret it. Since I have been helping to run the one here, I have found my last three full-time jobs because of it and tripled my salary! The Carl & Gary's Visual Basic Home Page has a very good listing of them.

List Servers

Another good place to obtain help is by joining a list server. The best way to describe a list sever is that it's a mail router. The way it works is that you send a Visual Basic question to the list server. The list server then sends it to everyone that is joined to it. So, you have potentially thousands of programmers reading your message. One hopes that at least one of them will know the solution to your problem. He responds to the list server with the answer so that you and all the others can read it.

This is a fantastic way to get your problems solved. I have been joined to the VISBAS-L list server group for many, many years. It has really help me out. Here os a list of some of the better ones and how to join them:

Visual Basic Forum (VISBAS-L)

This list deals with all Visual Basic programming issues. To subscribe, send e-mail to: listserv@peach.ease.lsoft.com

In the message, type:

```
sub VISBAS-L FirstName LastName
```

For example:

```
sub VISBAS-L David McCarter
```

Visual Basic Beginners Forum

This list is mainly for those new to Visual Basic.

To subscribe to the VISBAS-BEGINNERS list, simply write to LISTSERV@PEACH.EASE.LSOFT.COM and, in the text of your message (not the subject line), write:

```
SUBSCRIBE VISBAS-BEGINNERS
```

Newsgroups

Newsgroups are another good place to get information. Answers to questions often take a few days, though, because the news articles trickle out to servers around the world, and the answers trickle back over through the same, often slow, process. Here are couple popular Visual Basic newsgroups:

```
comp.lang.visual.basic.misc
comp.lang.visual.basic.3rdparty
```

Microsoft has also created a set of newsgroups that are becoming increasingly popular. All of the public Microsoft newsgroup names begin with microsoft.public, and the visual basic newsgroup names start with microsoft.public.Visual Basic.

Other Help

Microsoft Developers Network

MSDN is the official source from Microsoft for comprehensive programming information, development toolkits, and testing platforms. MSDN delivers all of this via a quarterly subscription, so our subscribers can be confident they're always working with the most up-to-date information and technology.

Depending on what level you join, each quarter you receive all the Microsoft documentation on CD-ROM, latest versions of all the different flavors of Windows and much, much more. It's a little costly, but well work it. It's a must for any development shop.

Contact MSDN.Call (800) 759-5474 department A622WEB, from 6:30 A.M. to 5:30 P.M. (Pacific time), Monday through Friday for subscription contents. Outside North America, contact your local Microsoft subsidiary, or call (510) 275-0763 in the U.S. to obtain local contact information.

Their website is located at http://www.microsoft.com/msdn

Index

3D, 15, 24, 25, 26, 140, 142

access, 34, 44, 108, 113, 114, 115, 116, 118, 124, 126, 133

activate, 6, 12

AddItem, 13, 22, 29, 30, 33, 35, 110

API, 2, 8, 12, 19, 30, 41, 42, 47, 49, 50, 54, 63, 65, 67, 75, 80, 81, 82, 87, 88, 90, 91, 92, 93, 94, 97, 99, 100, 103, 107, 110, 115, 125, 131, 132, 134, 151, 152

App.EXEName, 7, 68, 70

App.Path, 14, 55, 70, 79, 80, 81, 82, 114

App.PrevInstance, 6, 7, 12

AppActivate, 6

Appleman, 131, 151

array, 10, 11, 21, 22, 48

Asc, 8, 45, 84

ASCII, 8, 19

associated, 49, 64, 125, 128

automatic, 6

background, 65, 106

base, 19, 21

BBS, 133

beep, 7

book, 1, 2, 124, 130, 131, 145, 151, 152

books, 1, 2, 151

box, 18, 19, 53, 63, 71, 87, 124, 126, 128, 140, 143

button, 9, 16, 26, 64, 92, 103, 107, 127, 140

CD, 1, 153, 155

change, 2, 18, 28, 30, 80, 109, 127, 142, 146, 148

changing, 2, 28, 94

check, 30, 82, 83, 106, 114, 133, 134, 135, 136, 148, 149

checking, 81, 135

class, 12, 13

click, 9, 16, 71, 107, 132, 135

CMDIALOG.VBX, 50

color, 18, 26, 65

command, 75, 122, 140

COMMAND.COM, 88

COMMDLG.DLL, 39, 50, 51

CompactDatabase, 117

compacting, 116

CompuServe, 123, 131, 133

control, 6, 7, 9, 15, 16, 17, 18, 19, 26, 28, 30, 31, 34, 60, 68, 83, 92, 94, 109, 110, 116, 124, 125, 126, 132, 134, 142

controls, 9, 15, 23, 24, 25, 29, 32, 36, 92, 109, 119, 123, 124, 142, 152

Controls.Count, 25

CoTaskMemFree, 95, 96

create, 9, 19, 31, 34, 36, 41, 43, 47, 80, 129, 130, 135, 136

creating, 23, 63, 140, 148

Crescent, 139